LINCOLNSHIRE
FOLK
TALES

LINCOLNSHIRE
FOLK TALES

MAUREEN JAMES

The
History
Press

For all the Yellowbellies,
who I hope will appreciate and enjoy this book.

First published 2013

The History Press
The Mill, Brimscombe Port
Stroud, Gloucestershire, GL5 2QG
www.thehistorypress.co.uk

British Library Cataloguing in Publication Data.
A catalogue record for this book is available from the British Library.

ISBN 978 0 7524 6640 8

Typesetting and origination by The History Press
Printed in Great Britain by TJ International, Padstow, Cornwall.

CONTENTS

Acknowledgements

This book would not have been possible without the initial spark that lit the fire of my passion for history back in 1985, and for this I am grateful to both Barbara Johnson and Heather Falvey. I am also indebted to Liz Wright for persuading me that I could write professionally; Paul Jackson for showing me the power of the spoken story, and Del Reid for being a tower of strength for so many storytellers. I would also like to thank Rex Russell for inspiring not just me but many, many others in their love of local history, and Maureen Sutton for her tireless collection of Lincolnshire folklore. Numerous other storytellers and historians have also inspired me on my journey; these include Hugh Lupton, Malcolm Busby, Polly Howat, Graham Langley, Tim Davies, Ruairidh Greig, Mike Scott and Anne-Marie Taylor. Finally, I need to thank my husband Stuart, for helping with the illustrations, and he and the rest of my family for their patience and understanding.

INTRODUCTION

Like the other books within this series, this volume is a collection of folk tales linked to the landscape and to a specific
county. The county in this case is Lincolnshire, which is one of
the largest counties in England, and displays varied landscapes
as a result of its diverse geology: the clay, silt and peat of the
rivers flood plains Ancholme and Trent and the Fenland of the
south; the limestone that forms the Lincoln Cliff in the west;
the chalk and sandstone Wolds and finally the marshes to
the east.

THE WATER

Predominantly surrounded by water, the county has been heavily influenced by the river Trent to the west and the Humber
to the north, the long coastline to the east, which bounds the
North Sea, and the extensive Fen and Marshlands. The east
coast ports and the Humber Estuary encouraged trading

opportunities with Northern European countries, with the rivers providing the main communication links into and out of the area.

THE MARSHES

The boundary between Lincolnshire and the North Sea is protected by a coastal margin of magnificent sands which hold a peculiar charm. Moving inland, the long sand dunes, with their covering of marram grass and other plants, provide shelter for many species. Even further inland is the band of marshland, averaging about ten miles wide, from the Humber in the north to the Wash in the south. The Outmarsh, once subject to coastal erosion, has seen continual changes, and where once salt making was a major industry, recently the land has become eroded by ploughing. Now, farmers are being encouraged to abandon the arable crops in favour of grazing herds of cattle and haymaking in the small irregular fields bounded by dykes or drains. The Middle Marsh, a gently undulating platform that runs from the foot of the Lincolnshire Wolds to the Outmarsh, is characterised by rectilinear fields and occasional hedgerows.

THE WOLDS

Moving westwards, the limestone Wolds, a southern continuation of the Yorkshire Wolds, run for forty miles in a south-easterly direction from the Humber down to Spilsby on the eastern side of the county. The Wolds are about as wide as the level Marshland belt in most places, but north of Caistor the band reduces to less than five miles across. It also drops by Bametby-le-Wold to 150ft, to rise again near Elsham, so that by Saxby it reaches a height of 330ft, and remains at over 200ft until it reaches South Ferriby. Designated as an Area of Outstanding Natural Beauty, the Wolds shelter many villages and small towns within its folds or on the fringes.

The Cliff

In the west of the county and to the south of the city of Lincoln, the Lincoln Cliff, also known as the Lincolnshire Edge or Lincoln Heath, stretches for about seventy miles from the upper Humber at Winteringham down to Grantham and then to Stamford, breaking only where the River Witham carves its way through the limestone at Lincoln. The Cliff is much narrower than the Wolds it runs parallel to, and rises from Bottesford to Scunthorpe, reaching a height of 220ft near Burton-on-Stather, to descend dramatically by Alkborough to the Humber at Whitton.

The Carrs

Between the Wolds and the Cliff lie the Carrs, a belt of flatland that was once subject to frequent inundation. During the last ice age, twenty thousand years ago, this area was a glacial lake. After the ice sheet receded the area developed into a marshland with peat, in which ancient fallen trees, commonly known as bog oaks, have been found. As the sea level rose, the valley became a tidal estuary a few miles wide. The Romans chose the edge of this valley as the route for the great Ermine Street (now the A15), which ran from Newport Arch, at the north gate of Lincoln, arrow-straight to the Humber, near Winteringham. Once continuing on the other side of the Humber, the Lincolnshire stretch has now been diverted around Scampton and Broughton.

THE FENS

The flat landscape of the Fens in the south of the county has a special kind of beauty, with extended views, magnificent sunsets and 'big' skies. Fed by river floods and waters from the hills, the Fens were drained, with varying degrees of success, from medieval times. This enabled the area to raise cattle and sheep on summer pastures, and for the locals to become extremely wealthy. Successful year-round drainage did not occur until the nineteenth century, with the introduction of steam pumping engines. Now the land has been tilled to provide rich, flat farming land, with big straight-edged fields bounded by drainage ditches, or 'dykes', small and big, all interconnected and all carrying water to and from the bigger drains or rivers and thence to the sea. The soil, fine black peat and virtually free from stones, enables the growing of crops, particularly root vegetables, potatoes and sugar beet, in the abundant harvests.

THE ISLE OF AXHOLME

The Isle of Axholme can be found in the far north-west of the county. The name means 'The Island of Haxey', and it was the principal settlement in the area, and also the town made famous by the Haxey Hood Game. Originally, the landscape was one of wetlands, with villages and small towns sited on the higher ground. Today, the largely reclaimed area, like the fens further south, is dominated by a complex network of dykes, bridges and pumping stations.

BUT WHAT OF THE PEOPLE WHO TOLD THESE STORIES IN THE PAST, AND THE PEOPLE WHO COLLECTED THEM?

In the days before the invention of effective lighting, which led to longer working hours and the widespread availability of education, lessons would be taught, reminiscences would be shared and news would be spread by word of mouth. The long winter evenings would be times for sharing such tales whilst indoor tasks such as basketmaking, knitting, weaving and carding wool were carried out.

A Roger Ekirch noted that though many people could play a tune, often on a fiddle, it was found that storytelling was the night's principal entertainment; 'Legends, fables and tales of evils spirits, eternal stories recounted again and again by seasoned narrators with well-trained memories.'

The people would tell stories of things they believed in. Fred Kitchen, in his biography, reminisced about listening to the tales of a Lincolnshire man when he was a young boy living and working on farms in Nottinghamshire:

Harry would tell stories of witches. He was a 'Lincy', and his county seemed noted for witches and boggarts … if anyone had expressed a doubt about the truth of them, the whole company would have verified the truth by saying, 'I've eered my dad tell of 'im mony a time', or 'My grandfeyther ewsed to work on t'vary same plaice!' Indeed it was impossible to doubt, there were so many people who knew these people or 'knew people who knew these people'. It made a great impression on me, especially the witches and boggarts. Whenever I had to go along the dark lane to the village I thought of them. The conclusion I came to was that Yorkshire was a land of giants and blue-devils, Lincolnshire was over-run with witches and boggarts …

While living at Redbourne Vicarage, Marie Clothilde Balfour, who collected some of the stories included in this book in the late nineteenth century, described the setting for such storytelling within her novel *The Fall of the Sparrow*:

There were always people coming and going in the kitchen: women to fetch soup or wine for their sick, men smoking on the settle or drinking beer, the groom sleepily hissing as he polished an odd bit of harness, or a passing tramp warming himself at the fire, with a full plate balanced upon his knees, for there was beef and beer in plenty … And with the rattle of pewter and the steam rising fragrantly from the great pot … the voice of some old man monotonously crooning one of the ancient tales as it had been handed down to him from his fathers, tales of the strange things that walked in the Cars; amid the mists, in the evil hours of darkness.

As people became literate they began to regard the traditional popular pastimes as belonging to a different world than that of their own, and the schoolmasters, HM Inspectors of Schools and the clergy openly discouraged superstitious beliefs. Thankfully, many people recognised that these actions could lead to a complete loss of an important part of the cultural history of this land and they diligently recorded (and also transformed or even suppressed) the old stories 'according to personal tastes and circumstances'.

The folktale collectors who recorded the songs, stories and traditions that have been passed down to us in fairy tales, nursery rhymes and playground games also discovered 'that the inhabitants of rural England had not abandoned their faith in healing wells, divination, cunning folk, witch-craft, omens or ghosts'.

Whilst the collectors went about their business within the communities, the competition from newspapers and books containing informative accounts of current affairs began to eclipse storytelling in importance, particularly in the more populated areas. Storytelling was seen as the entertainment for the very old, or the very young, but at what loss?

Author Beverley Nichols noted in 1934 that 'the mysteries have gone. We know what lies on the other side of the hill. The scientists have long ago puffed out, scorn-fully, the golden lamp of the night … leaving us in the utmost darkness …'

Fortunately, many of the ancient stories were preserved and there has recently been a resurgence of interest in stories and storytelling. Simon Heywood, well-known folklor-ist and scholar of traditional storytelling, noted a number of loosely coherent movements in England and Wales 'in the arts, education, and culture at all levels … wherein the ever present but resurgent appetite for the many forms of spoken story can be focused, fed and stimulated'.

ABOUT THIS BOOK

This re-emergence of interest in one of the oldest art forms has directly influenced this series by The History Press. For their authors they have requested people who *tell* stories rather than read them, and those who have a deep interest in their respective counties.

I hope that I fulfil this aim within this volume, but I don't want to be the only one to take credit for passing these tales on to you. I would also like to follow the example of the folk tale collectors in the past, and give you some background information of these people, and also, where possible, information on the actual tellers.

Gervase Holles (1607–1675) was collecting popular antiquities, later to be known as folklore, long before the latter word was even devised. Born in Grimsby, he was a prominent Royalist and a lawyer. He served as Mayor of Grimsby and MP for the town before and after the English Civil War.

Abraham de la Pryme (1671–1704) was also an antiquarian. Born in Hatfield, on the Levels near Doncaster, he became a curate in Broughton and then Hull. He kept a diary – *Ephemeri Vitae: A Diary of My Own Life* – from the age of twelve until his death, in which he recorded items of interest.

George Stovin (1696–1780) was born at Tetley Hall, in the parish of Crowle, and lived the life of a country

gentleman. His main interest was research of the topography
and antiquities of the area of his birth. He was particularly
interested in the drainage of the Level of Hatfield Chase,
where he had inherited estates. It was said that he rarely left
the Levels, regarding 'No part of England comparable to the
Isle of Axholme, and no town equal to Crowle'. Later in life,
however, he did cross the Trent and took up residence in
Winterton, 'In a little cottage which he had made Arcadian
with honeysuckles and other flowers, where he was to be
seen with his pipe every morning at five, and where he was
accustomed to amuse his neighbours with the variety of
anecdote with which his memory supplied him.'

Henry Evan Smith (1828–1908) was a local correspond-
ent for the *Stamford Mercury*, *North Lincolnshire Star* and
other papers. He left numerous manuscript notes, many of
which are now in the Lincolnshire Archives.

James Conway Walter (1831–1913), the eldest son
of a Lincolnshire clergyman, was born in Langton near
Horncastle. He went to Cambridge University and
became vicar of St Andrews, Langton (Woodhall Spa) and
Kirkstead, Lincolnshire, in 1869. After twenty-one years
he relinquished the latter position and became rector at
Langton. During his career he became a highly respected
Lincolnshire historian, and wrote a number of books and
papers on Lincolnshire history, including 'The Legend of
Bayards Leap' which was included in *Bygone Lincolnshire*
(1891). He also contributed various items on folklore
to Mabel Peacock, including the script to a rather bawdy
Lincolnshire plough play that had been performed in the
kitchen of his rectory about the year 1889.

Edward Peacock (1831–1915) was the only son of
Edward Shaw Peacock, a wealthy Lincolnshire landowner

and agriculturalist. The young Edward was educated at home and developed an interest in history and archaeology. He lived at Bottesford Manor House, situated on the outskirts of modern Scunthorpe. He married Lucy Anne Wetherell from America and the couple had six children. After the death of his wife in 1887, and due to financial pressures, Edward and his daughter Mabel moved to Dunstan House, Kirton in Lindsey. He was an avid collector of folklore, which he sent to various publications, including local newspapers. He was also collecting evidence for *The Folklore of Lincolnshire*, a task that was eventually completed by his daughter. Throughout his life, Edward researched the Lincolnshire dialect, and he continued submitting short items to *Folklore* until 1908. He also wrote four novels, none of which were particularly successful.

Mabel Geraldine Woodruffe Peacock (1856–1920) followed on from the work of her father in submitting papers and notes to *Folklore* between 1887 and 1917, quite a number of which were based on Lincolnshire folklore. She published three collections of stories and verse, *Tales and Rhymes in Lindsey Folk-Speech* (1886), *Taales fra Linkisheere* (1889) and *Lincolnshire Tales: The Recollections of Eli Twigg* (1897), which include a number of Lincolnshire versions of traditional tales and rhymes telling stories of boggarts, fairies and fools. In 1902, she commenced correspondence with the Folklore Society on the subject of taking over from her father in the collection of Lincolnshire folklore. This work, which was carried out with Mrs Gutch, was completed and published in 1908. Mabel did not collect folklore in the field; indeed, a neighbour is recorded as saying that she rarely left her house, but gleaned information from friends and acquaintances.

Robert Marshall Heanley (1848–1915), the eldest son of a wealthy farmer, was born in Croft in the south-east of the county. He entered the Church in 1875 and became assistant curate at Burgh-le-Marsh before becoming rector of Wainfleet All Saints and perpetual curate of Wainfleet St Thomas until 1889. His parishes were close to the place of his birth, which, along with boyhood memories, he drew on to produce pieces on Marshland folklore for *Lincolnshire Notes and Queries* (1891), for *Folklore* (1898) and for an article on 'The Vikings: Traces of their Folklore in Marshland' for the *Saga Book of the Viking Club* (1903).

James Alpass Penny (1855–1944) was born in Crewkerne, Somerset, where his father was headmaster of the grammar school. He became the vicar of Stixwould, a village near Horncastle, in 1888. Seven years later he moved five miles to become the vicar of Wispington. Suffering from blindness, he spent his later years at Woodhall Spa, also in the Horncastle area. He produced two collections of folklore from around the locality, which also included popular memories and incidents from his own experience as a parish clergyman.

Willingham Franklin Rawnsley (1845–1927), born in Hertfordshire, was the eldest son of the rector of Halton Holgate, Lincolnshire. William's brother, Canon Hardwicke Drummond Rawnsley, was one of the founders of the National Trust, and it was through this connection that Willingham developed an interest in the environment. Though he was the proprietor of Winton House, a private school in Winchester, for a number of years and spent his retirement in Guildford, he kept his interest in the county of his ancestors, as evidenced in his travel book *The Highways and Byways of Lincolnshire* (1914). He was also related by marriage to Tennyson, and was an expert on his poems.

Sidney Oldall Addy (1848–1933) was an antiquary and man of letters. Born at Norton, Derbyshire, he was the son of a colliery owner, and studied Classics at Lincoln College, Oxford. He became a solicitor and spent much of his life in Sheffield, combining his work with his other interests. He wrote a number of books, including a collection of tales from *Household Tales with other Traditional Remains Collected in the Counties of York, Lincoln, and Derby*, in the introduction to which he noted that 'The ancient stories, beautiful or highly humorous even in their decay, linger with us here and there in England, and, like rare plants, may be found by those who seek them'. He collected all the tales from the oral tradition rather than printed sources, and wrote them up using the words of the narrator, but without the dialect and with the exception of obsolete words.

Marie Clothilde Balfour (1862–1931) was born in Edinburgh, but spent some of her childhood in New Zealand. She was a cousin of Robert Louis Stevenson, and in 1885 she married another of her cousins, James Craig Balfour, a physician and surgeon. Between 1887 and 1889 the couple lived in the vicarage at Redbourne, North Lincolnshire, where Marie collected a number of stories from the local people. A description of this experience was included in a semi-biographical novel and outlined earlier in this introduction.

The first of the tales collected by Marie was included by Andrew Lang in both *Longman's Magazine* and *Folklore*, the journal of the Folklore Society. This received a favourable reaction and probably prompted her to send the collection of 'Legends of the Carrs' to the society. They were included in *Folklore* in three parts in 1891, but sadly, Marie was not skilled in dialect though she attempted to record the tales accurately. This misguided attempt probably led to later criticism of the authenticity of the stories, but an investigation by myself, into their content, and the views of people from the area, leads me to conclude that they were indeed from the Lincolnshire Carrs. I have included eight of the stories collected by Marie, in this book. For each I have 'translated' them from the original dialect and carried out a minimum amount of editing.

Leland Lewis Duncan (1862–1923) was born in Kent and became a life member of the Kent Archaeological Society. He was made a Fellow of the Society of Antiquaries in London in 1890.

Ethel H. Rudkin (1893–1985) followed in the footsteps of Mabel Peacock. Indeed, she recalled visits made as a child with her parents to Kirton in Lindsey, home of the Peacocks. Born Ethel Hutchinson in Willoughton, Lincolnshire, her mother's family were the Pickthalls of Suffolk. An only child, she was educated in Scarborough before gaining employment as a governess. In 1914, whilst at a point-to-point meeting at Burton near Lincoln, she met George Rudkin, who she married three years later. George served in the war, firstly in the Yeomanry and then as a Lieutenant in the Machine Gun Corps. Sadly, he died on 28 October 1918 from the influenza epidemic that is believed to have killed 250,000 people in Britain and millions worldwide. His mother died on the same day. As his widow, Ethel gained George's share in the Rudkin family farm and for a time she helped in this venture. By 1927, she had returned to live with her parents in Willoughton, where she stayed to look after them in their old age. A devoted, and lifelong collector of Lincolnshire oral history and folklore, she travelled up and down the county in the 1920s and '30s, in a bull-nosed Morris car, collecting evidence directly from the rural villagers on a broad range of topics. She submitted a number of articles to *Folklore* and produced a book, *Lincolnshire Folklore*, which was published at her own expense in 1936. The preface to the book stated that everything in it was 'authentic and collected between World War One and Two from people not books'. Ethel also had a keen interest in archaeology, local and social history and dialect, and eventually became an acknowledged expert in all these subjects within the county. Her home became a place of pilgrimage for researchers wishing to view an enormous quantity of books, manuscripts, artefacts, memorabilia and farm implements, and to also enjoy a cup of tea with the lively lady herself. In the 1970s, Ethel moved to a cottage in Toynton All Saints where she spent the remaining years of her life. She was instrumental in cataloguing the vast collection of artefacts that formed the core of the Museum of Lincolnshire Life and much of her personal collection was donated to the Lincolnshire Museum Service after her death.

Ruth Lyndall Tongue (1898–1981) is normally regarded as a Somerset folklorist, though she was born in Staffordshire. Her mother, Betsy Mabel Jones, was from Whitchurch, Shropshire, but her father, a Congregational Minster, had been born in Louth, Lincolnshire, and both of his parents and grandparents were natives of the county. Ruth recalled hearing stories from her aunt, Annie Tongue, in Alkborough, and from her great-aunt, Hetty Carr of Blyton Farm, near Gainsborough. Annie Tongue, Ruth said, had heard stories from her female ancestors who were also born and raised in Lincolnshire.

So why are Lincolnshire people called Yellowbellies? The subject is being continually debated, and a number of conclusions have been reached, the most popular being the following: the officers of the Royal North Lincolnshire Militia and the old Lincolnshire Regiment wore yellow as part of their uniform; opium taken for the marsh fever (or ague), and the fever itself, would turn the skin yellow; a creature, such as a frog or eel, commonly found in the county had a yellow underbelly, and finally that the Lincolnshire mail coaches used to have yellow bodywork.

Maureen James, 2013

Alkborough
Winterton
Outer Marsh
East Halton
Isle
of
Axholme
High Risby
Scunthorpe
Grimsby
Wroot
Hibaldstow
Caistor
Haxey
Redbourne
Inner
Marsh
Clays
Blyton
Clays
Wold
Outer
Marsh
Gainsborough
Louth
Cliff
Pilford Bridge
Buslingthorpe
Wold
Mumby
Saxilby
Stainfield
Lincoln
Horncastle
Clays
Hykeham
Fens
Kirkstead
Heath
Tattershall
Anwick
Cranwell
Langrick
Clays
Sleaford
Swineshead
Fens
Heath
Holbeach
Fens
Crowland
Heath

1

OF SIGNIFICANT
STONES

There are many stories found in Lincolnshire relating to specific stones and this section includes just a few of them. The first is the tale of Grim and Boundel, and the two stones they stole from the Danes to help the people of Lindsey to prosper. The tale is told, more or less, as it was collected in the first half of the nineteenth century by Henry Evan Smith of Caistor, 'from conversations with several old residents, rustics of the neighbourhood'. The second explores the many tales of William the Hermit of Lindholme and Tommy Lindum of Wroot. Both names are interchangeable, though the former site is just over the border in Yorkshire. This is followed by the tale of 'Yallery Brown', which is less well known, probably because it does not relate to a specific site, though it has been set within the landscape of the north of the county. The tales of the 'Fonaby Sack Stone' and the 'Anwick Drake Stone(s)' complete the section, both being accounts of the origins of real stones.

GRIM AND BOUNDEL

A long time ago, they say it was before the Danes first came to Lindsey, there was a man they called Little Grim, but a big man he was, and a great sea captain like his forefathers. This Grim used to sail about to foreign parts and sometimes fought and sometimes traded with the foreign folks. It was on one of his voyages that he heard tell of two magic stones belonging to the King of the Danes, and how, whenever they were beaten with hazel rods, this would make the rain fall and the grass grow and cows prosper and everything be plentiful. At that time there was a drought and almost famine in this country.

So Grim thought to himself that he would steal these stones and bring them home with him. He and his best man, Boundel, who was as big as he was, went ashore after dark, and shouldering a stone each, carried them off to his ship. Then a strange thing happened – the ship began sinking as soon as the stones were on board, and they had to throw everything overboard to keep afloat. And so, with water up to the gunwale, they made the voyage home.

They say it was at Tetney that Grim landed, and from there he wanted to send the stones to King Lud, but then nobody but him and his man Boundel could lift them. So they shouldered them again and set off for the royal town.

The stones seemed to get heavier and heavier until they got to Grainsby Bridge, which broke under Grim and he began to sink into the mud (there was little water in the Old Fleet then). Boundel had gone over first and was resting in Thoresby, so he went back and helped Grim out with his load. Grim went on till he came to Audleby, where he stayed to rest, but the stones never went further, for neither Grim nor Boundel could ever lift them again.

So much the better for the men of the Wolds and the Marsh. Boundel told them the secret of the magic the stones possessed, and the stones were beaten – Boundel's for rain, and Grim's to make the corn grow – till there was plenty in the land. Every year for a long while after, folks came from far and wide to eat a grand feast around the stones, which were whipped till everybody prospered. But then the Devil came and flew away with Grim's stone.

When asked about the truth of the legend of Grim and Boundel, the local people would point out that there were places in the locality called Grim's Croft and Boundel's Croft at which the stones were once seen. It has also been noted that the custom of 'Beating the Bounds', during which the parish boundary would be walked to check that all was in order, included the beating of stones with a stick or stripped willow wands.

Researchers have theorised that Grim's Stone was located at North Thoresby and for a time separated the parish of Clee from the borough of Grimsby. Today, it sits along-side the Havelok Stone, which used to separate the parish of Wellow from the borough of Grimsby, outside the Welholme Galleries.

WILLIAM THE HERMIT OF LINDHOLME AND TOMMY LINDUM OF WROOT

On the border of North Lincolnshire and South Yorkshire is a low-lying area that was often flooded. The land,

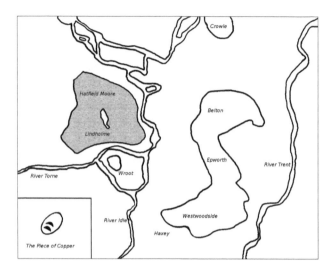

once known as the Hatfield or Turf Moor, had in its centre a piece of land of about sixty acres that was raised higher than the rest and at the centre of this piece of land there once stood a solitary farmhouse. This spot was known as Lindholme, and it was once the abode of William the Hermit.

> Within an humble lonesome cell
> He free from care and noise does dwell,
> No pomp, no pride, no cursed strife,
> Disturbs the quiet of his life.
> (Abraham de la Pryme)

In a fifteenth-century description, William is said to wear 'strange skins' with the pelt on the inside and the fur next to his skin. Under this he wore a tunic and leg garments both bound to his body with twine made from rushes. He also had a plaited girdle around his waist from which hung a knife, a hook and an axe. On his head he wore a fur cap over his long matted hair, the latter blending with his long matted beard.

The Crowle antiquarian George Stovin visited the site and sent a report to the *Gentleman's Magazine* in 1727 (along with a sketch of the beaten piece of copper mentioned in the text):

> The people of Hatfield and places adjacent have a tradition, that on the middle of Hatfield waste there formerly lived an ancient Hermit who was called William of Lindholme; he was by the common people taken for a cunning man or conjurer, but in order to be better informed I, accompanied with the Rev. Mr Sam Wesley, and others, went to view the place, and after passing the morass, found the hermitage or cell situate in the middle of 60 acres of firm sandy ground full of pebbles, on which was growing barley, oats, and peas. There was likewise a well 4 or 5 yards deep, full of clear spring water, which is very remarkable, because the water of the morass is of the colour of coffee. Here is great plenty of furze bushes etc. and variety of game, such as hares, foxes, kites, eagles, curlews, ducks and geese: there is no house or cottage near it, and but a few old oaks, fallows, and birch; the house is a little stud-bound one, and seems ready to fall. At the east end stood an altar made of hewn stone, and at the west is the Hermit's grave covered with a free stone that measures in length 8 foot and a half, in breadth 3, and in thickness 8, which with the content of Richard Howlegate the present inhabitant, and the help of levers we raised up, and removed; and digging under found a tooth, a scull, the thigh and shin bones of a human body, all of a very large size; we likewise found in the grave a peck of hemp seed, and a beaten piece of copper. It is difficult to imagine how such vast stones should be brought, when

it's even difficult for man or horse to travel over the morass, which in some places is 4 miles cross, on which grows an odoriferous herb called gale, and a plant named silk or cotton grass from its white tuff on the top resembling the finest cotton wool; it is supposed before the draining the levels of Hatfield that there was plenty of water by which the great stones must have been conveyed, this I think the most probable conjecture.

Stovin was concerned about the facts of the site, but Abraham de la Pryme wrote in his diary on the folk traditions of the place. He quoted a comparison of William of Lindholme and Shakespeare's Prospero, adding that he must have been in league with 'infernal spirits' as he had strength beyond that of an ordinary man. He also noted that among the many traditional stories concerning him there is:

One to the effect that, when he was a boy, his parents went to Wroot feast, and left him to keep the sparrows from the corn or hemp seed … he drove all the sparrows into a barn, which was then being built, and still un roofed, and confined them there by placing a harrow against the door. After he had done this, he followed his parents to Wroot; and when scolded for so doing, said he had fastened up all the sparrows in a barn. They went home and found the sparrows all dead, except a few which were turned white. Since this transaction it is said that no sparrows were ever seen at Lindholme.

Mabel Peacock compared William of Lindholme to the Irish Fann MacCuil [*sic*], and also related the story of how when William was asked to keep the sparrows off the land, he was so annoyed that he threw an enormous stone at the house to which his parents had gone. He threw the stone too high and it fell on the further side of the building. The farmer, on whose field it had landed, yoked six horses to it but despite their combined strength they failed in their task to move it and all died soon after. For many years it was considered unlucky to meddle with this stone or with the other large stones in the district. Two such stones, the 'thumb stone' and the 'little finger-stone', were believed to have also been thrown by William.

Mabel also noted a tale of how it was very wet one day as William was going from Lindholme to Hatfield and he said that he would make a road if a rider on a horse would gallop the distance without looking behind him. A rider agreed to do this, considering it to be an easy task. However, as he rode, the noise behind him was so awful that he had to look round. He saw stones and gravel flying in all directions as little demons in red jackets were macadamising the road as fast as they could. 'God speed your work!' yelled the terrified rider, as he rode on as fast as he could. The work immediately stopped, and it is said that the road remained unfinished for another two hundred years.

A similar tale has also been recorded, with William as the rider and the pixy king as the one who said he would make the road.

William also became connected to the story of how he was told to fetch some straw from a neighbour. The latter told him to take as much as he could carry, and he stuck his fork in a whole stack and carried that home.

A story is also told of William's death and how leading up to it:

As the infirmities of age grew upon him, and he was warned of death's approach, he dug for himself a grave, beneath the floor of his cell, and provided a large stone for its cover. This he propped up, in a leaning position over the hole, with a piece of wood. When death's hand seemed to be upon him, he laid himself down in his self-made grave, and, by a string attached to the prop of the stone, he pulled it away, and allowed the stone to drop into its place and cover him, and thus became, not only his own grave-digger, but his own sexton also.

Ethel Rudkin recorded in her diary (1930) that she was told the stories of Tommy Lindum (or Lindrum) of Wroot, by a man driving cows near Wroot village. These stories were the same as the tales of William of Lindholme. The man added that he had seen the beginning of a cobbled road that was made by 'Tommy' and an old box at Lindholme in the granary that contained his bones. She managed to see the stones connected to the hermit.

YALLERY BROWN

I've heard tell that the bogles and boggarts were really bad in the old times, but I can't rightly say as I've never seen any myself; not rightly bogles, that is, but I'll tell you about Yallery Brown – if he wasn't a boggart he was very similar, and I know this myself. It's all true; strange and true.

I was working on the High Farm then and just a lad of sixteen or maybe eighteen years – and my mother and folks dwelt down by the pond yonder, at the far end of the village. I had the stables and such to see to, and the horses to help with and odd jobs to do, and the work was hard but the pay good. I reckon I was an idle scamp, for I couldn't abide hard work and I looked forward all the week to Sundays, when I had to walk down home and not go back till twilight. By the green lane I could get to the farm in a matter of twenty minutes, but there used to be a path across the west field yonder, by the side of the spinney, and on past the fox covert and so to the ramper. I used to go that way, for it was longer for one thing, and I was never in a hurry to get back to the work, and it was still pleasant like on summer nights out in the broad silent fields, midst the smell of growing things. Folk said that the spinney was haunted, and for sure I had seen lots of fairy stones and rings and that along the grass edge; but I had never seen anything in the way of horrors and boggarts, let alone Yallery Brown before.

One Sunday I walked across the west field on a beautiful July night. It was warm and still and the air was full of little sounds as though the trees and grass were chattering to themselves. And all at once there came from ahead of me the most pitiful crying I have ever heard, sob, sobbing, like a frightened baby, and near heartbroken, breaking off into a moan and then rising again in a long whimpering wailing that made me feel sick to listen to it. I was always fond of babies, too, and I began to look everywhere for the poor creature. 'Must be Sally Bratton's,' I thought to myself, 'she was always a flighty thing and never looked after the brat. Like as not she's flaunting about the lanes and has clean forgot the baby.' But though I looked and looked, I could see nothing. Nevertheless, the sobbing was at my very ear, so tired like and sorrowful that I kept crying out, 'Shush bairn, shush! I'll take you back to your mother if you'll only shush your crying.'

But for all my looking I could not find the baby. I looked under the hedge by the spinney side, and I climbed over it and I sought up and down and in the middle of the trees, and through the long grass and weeds, but I only frightened some sleeping birds and stung my own hands with the nettles. I found nothing, and I nearly gave up and stood there scratching my head, clearly beaten by it all, and presently the whimpering got louder and stronger in the quietness, and I thought I could make out words of some sort. I listened with all my ears, and the sorry thing was saying all mixed up with sobbing, 'Oh! The stone, the great big stone! Oh! Oh! The stone on top!'

Naturally, I wondered where the stone might be, and I looked again. There by the hedge bottom was a great flat stone, nearly buried in the mools and hidden by the tangled grass and weeds; one of the stones that we used to call the 'Stranger's Tables'. Down I fell on my knee-bones by the stone, and listened again. Clearer than ever, but tired and spent with crying, came the little sobbing voice, 'Oh! Oh! The stone, the stone on top!'

I was getting concerned about meddling with the thing, but I couldn't stand the whimpering, and I tore like mad at the stone till I felt it lifting from the mools, and all at once it came with a sigh, out of the damp earth and the tangled grass and growing things. And there in the hole lay a tiddy thing on his back, blinking up at the moon and at me. It was no bigger than a year-old brat, but had long tangled hair and beard twisted round its body so I couldn't see its clothes, and the hair was all yellow and shining and silky, like a bairn's, but the face – it was old as if it was hundreds of years since it was young and smooth; just a heap of wrinkles and two bright black eyes in the middle, set in a lot of shining yellow hair. The skin was the colour of the fresh turned earth in the spring – brown as brown could be – and his bare hands and feet were brown like its face. The crying stopped, but the tears were standing on its cheeks, and the tiddy thing looked bewildered like the moonshine in the night air. I was wondering what I'd do, but by and by he scrambled out of the hole, and stood looking about him. He wasn't up to my knee, but he was the queerest creature I have ever set eyes on. Brown and yellow all over, with such a glint in his eye and such a wizened face that I felt afraid of him, even though he was so tiddy and old.

The creature's eyes soon got used to the moonlight, and presently it looked up in my face as bold as ever. 'Tom,' says he, 'you're a good lad! Tom, you're a good lad!' and his voice was soft and high and piping like a little bird twittering.

I touched my hat and began to think what I should say, but I was frozen with fear and I couldn't open my gob.

'Houts!' says the thing again, 'you needn't be afraid of me; you've helped me more than you know, my lad, and I'll do as much for you.' I couldn't speak yet but I thought, 'Lord! For sure it is a bogle!'

'No,' says he as quick as quick, 'I'm not a bogle, but you'd best not ask me what I am; anyway I'm a good friend of yours.'

My very knee-bones struck, for certainly any ordinary body could not have known what I had been thinking to

myself, but he looked so kind like, and spoke so fair, that I made bold to get out, a bit quavery like, 'Might I be asking to know your honour's name?'

'Hmm,' says he, pulling his beard, 'as for that …' and he thought a bit. 'Ay so,' he went on at last, 'Yallery Brown, Tom, Yallery Brown's your friend, my lad.'

'Thank you, master', says I, quite meek like.

'Ah now,' he says, 'I'm in a hurry tonight, but tell me quick, what will I do for you? Will you have a wife? I can give you the rampinest lass in the town. Will you be rich? I'll give you gold as much as you can carry; or will you have help with your work? Only say the word.'

I scratched my head. 'Well as for a wife, I have no desire for such; they're but bothersome bodies, and I have women-folk at home that will mend my clothes; and for gold that's as may be', for you see I thought he was talking only; and maybe he couldn't do as much as he said. 'But for work, there, I can't abide work, and if you will give me a helping hand with it I'll thank – '

'Stop,' says he, quick as lightning, 'I'll help you and wel-come, but if ever you say that to me – if ever you thank me, do you see? You'll never see me again. Remember that now; I want no thanks, I'll have no thanks, do you hear?' and he stamped his tiddy foot on the earth and looked as wicked as a raging bull.

'Remember that now,' he went on calming down a bit, 'and if you need help, or gets into trouble, call on me and just say, "Yallery Brown come from the mools, I want you!" and I'll be with you at once. And now,' says he, picking a dandelion puff, 'goodnight!' and he blew it up, and it all came in my eyes and ears. Soon as I could see again the tiddy creature was gone, and but for the stone on end and the hole at my feet I'd thought I'd been dreaming.

I went home and to bed, and by the morning I'd nearly forgot all about him. But when I went to the work, there were none to do! All was done already: the horses seen to, the stables cleaned out, everything in its proper place, and I'd nowt to do but sit with my hands in my pockets. And so it went on day after day, all the work done by Yallery Brown, and better done, too, than I could have done it myself. If the master gave me more work, I sat down and the work did itself, the singing irons and the broom set to, with never a hand put to them.

I never saw Yallery Brown in daylight; only in the twilight I saw him hopping about like a will-o-the-wyke without his lantern.

At first it was good for me, I'd nowt to do and good pay for it. But by and by, things began to go arsy-varsy. If the work was done for me, it was undone for the other lads; if my buckets were filled, theirs were upset; if my tools were sharpened, theirs were blunted and spoiled; if my horses were clean as daisies, theirs were splashed with muck, and so on – day in and day out, it was always the same. And the lads saw Yallery Brown flitting about of nights, and they saw the thing working without hands in daylight, and they saw that my work was done for me, and theirs was undone for them; and naturally they begun to be wary of me, and they wouldn't speak or come near me, and they carried tales to the master and so things went from bad to worse.

For, you see, I could do nothing myself; the brooms wouldn't stay in my hand, the plough ran away from me, the hoe kept out of my grip. I'd thought often that I would do my own work after all, so maybe Yallery Brown would leave me and my neighbours alone. But I couldn't – true as death I couldn't. I could only sit by and look on, and have the cold shoulder turned on me, while the unnatural thing was meddling with the others and working for me.

At last, things got so bad that the master gave me the sack, and if he hadn't, I do believe that all the rest of the lads would have sacked him, for they swore that they would not stay on the same yard as me. Well naturally I felt bad – it was a very good place and good pay too – and I was very angry with Yallery Brown, as he'd got me into such trouble. So before I knew it I shook my fist in the air and called out as loud as I could 'Yallery Brown, come from the mools, you scamp, I want you!'

You'd scarce believe it, but I had hardly brought out the words, when I felt something tweaking my leg from behind and I jumped with the suddenness of it; and as soon as I looked down, there was the tiddy thing, with his shining hair, and wrinkled face, and wicked glinting black eyes.

He was in a fine rage, and I would like to have kicked him, but it would do no good for there wasn't enough of him to get my boot against, but I said at once, 'Look here master, I'll thank you to leave me alone after this, do you hear? I want none of your help, and I'll have nothing more to do with you – do you see?'

The horrid thing broke out with a screeching laugh, and pointed his brown finger at me. 'Ho, ho, Tom!' says he. 'You thanked me, my lad, and I told you not to, I told you not to!'

'I don't want your help, I tell you!' I yelled at him 'I only want never to see you again, and to have nowt more to do with you – you can go – ' but I won't tell you all I said, for I was very angry.

The thing only laughed and screeched and mocked as long as I went on swearing, but soon my breath ran out.

'Tom, my lad,' he said with a grin, 'I'll tell you some-thing, Tom. True as true I'll never help you again and call though you will, you'll never see me after today; but I never said I would leave you alone, Tom, and I never will my lad! I was nice and safe under the stone, Tom, and could do no harm; but you let me out yourself, and you can't put me back again! I would have been your friend and work for you if you had been wise; but since you are no more than a born fool, I'll give you no more than a born fool's luck; and when all goes arsy-varsy, you'll remember that its Yallery Brown's doing; though you won't see me. Mark my words will you?'

And he began to sing, dancing round me like a bairn with yellow hair, but looking older than ever, with his grinning wrinkled bit of a face:

Work as thou will, thou'll never do well,
Work as thou might, thou'll never gain owt;
For harm and mischance and Yallery Brown
You let out yourself from under the stone.

Ay, he said those very words, and they have rung in my ears ever since, over and over again, like a bell tolling for the bur-ying, and it was the burying of my luck – for I never had any since. However, the imp stood there mocking and grinning at me, and chuckling like the old devil's own wicked self.

And, man! I can't rightly remember what he said next. It was all cursing and calling down misfortune on me; but I was so amazed with fright that I could only stand there, shaking all over and staring down at the horrid thing. I reckon if he'd gone on longer, I'd have tumbled down in a fit. But by and by, his yellow shining hair rose up in the air and wrapped itself round me, so it looked to all the world like a great dandelion puff; and he floated away on the wind over the wall and out of sight, with a parting skirl of his wicked voice and sneering laugh.

I can tell you, I was nearly dead with fear, and I can scarcely say how I got home.

Well, that's my tale, and it's true, every word of it, and there are others beside me that have seen Yallery Brown and know his evil tricks, and did it come? My word, but it did, sure as death! I have worked here and there, and turned my hand to this and that, but it always went wrong, and it's all Yallery Brown's doing. I'm getting old now, and I must end my days in the workhouse I reckon, but until I am dead and buried, and perhaps even afterwards, there'll be no end to Yallery Brown's spite at me; and day in, day out I hear him saying while I sit here trembling:

> Work as thou will, thou'll never do well
> Work as thou might, thou'll never gain owt;
> For harm and mischance and Yallery Brown
> You let out yourself from under the stone.

The landscape of the tale reflects the geography of the village of Redbourne, where there is a farm known locally as High Farm up on the other side of the ramper and there is a pond in the village. Marie Balfour collected the story and it is likely that the tale may have been adapted by the teller, who I believe to be Thomas Lamming, whilst he was employed as a labourer and living at Staniwells Farm, Hibaldstow.

Though Katharine Briggs felt that the tale resembled a story from the Welsh Marches, in which a young man made offerings to the fairies to gain help with making his sweetheart his wife. His wish came true, but his wife was a scold and soon died and his luck turned bad, it is my belief that it is also close to the story of the Hob Thrust found at East Halton.

As regards to the description of the Yallery Brown, he bears a resemblance to the 'pygmy being, man-like with long hair and the face of a seal' that was once believed to cross the River Trent at Jenny Hurn in a little coracle. Also, regarding creatures living under stones, Ethel Rudkin found evidence of belief that the devil lived beneath stones at Helmswell, Spring Hills and at Winceby.

I also believe that the story has links with the folklore connected to Tommy Lindum (or William of Lindholme) as he was buried under a stone. Similarly, in the tale of 'The Dead Moon', also collected in Redbourne, the moon is trapped under a stone. Both of these stories, and 'The Hob Thrust', are included within this book.

FONABY SACK STONE

At Fonaby Top, not far from Caistor on the road to Grimsby, there are a group of stones known collectively as the Sack Stone, or the Fonaby Stone. The stone originally stood in the middle of the field at the top of the hill and comprised three piled stones, the top one of which resembled an open sack with a band around the neck.

It was said that a stranger to the area was riding along the track over the Wolds when he saw a man sewing grain. The rider stopped to ask the man if he would give, or sell, him some of the grain for his horse, but the man said, 'I am short of corn myself, and can neither give nor sell.'

The stranger looked at a full sack of corn close by and said, 'You still have a full sack, and you have almost finished sowing. I need some corn for my horse.'

'That is not a sack of corn,' said the man, 'it is a great cobble stone.'

At this response, the rider became angry and uttered the following curse:

Saints reward both thee and thine,
As thou rewardest me and mine.
A stone, thou sayest, I can see –
Stone for ever shall it be!

As he said this, the sack of corn did indeed turn to stone, and there it remained, through wind and weather for many years until it was moved. But there is a curse attached to the stone if it is moved.

It is said that a farmer once, against the advice of the older and wiser people in the community, decided to move the stone down the hill to the yard. He put together a team of horses and tried to drag the stone so that it was not in the way of ploughing but they failed in the task. He then yoked the bullocks to the stone and tried again, and slowly they dragged the stone down to the yard.

Once he had moved the stone, the curse started to work. First his horses and then his bullocks became sick and died. Then his eldest son was also taken ill, and everyone said it was 'the old stone'. They all agreed that until the stone was returned to its former position nothing would thrive.

The farmer decided that rather than risk using any good animals on the task, he would get the farm boy to use the old lame mare to pull the stone. The boy did this and they were all surprised to see the stone almost make its own way up the hill. After that, the bad luck of the farmer ceased.

Rudkin found that over the years other people had tried to move the stone, and either suffered bad luck or perished. However, after the stone split into three, the pieces were moved to the west hedge side with no ill effects. The power had gone.

The same story is also told as set in the seventh century, with St Paulinus of York riding an ass past the field. Similarly, a version has been found about Jesus Christ coming to Caistor and asking the farmer for some bread. The farmer could only provide one loaf, and so Christ turned some stones into barley.

The Sack Stone is now on private land, and only two pieces of the moss-covered stone remain.

The Anwick Drake Stone(s)

Outside the main entrance to the parish churchyard in the village of Anwick, there can be seen the Drake Stones which were believed to be associated with the devil. In 1833, *The Gentleman's Magazine* printed the following account from the antiquarian Dr George Oliver:

> It is said that the devil's cave is under this stone, and that it contains hidden treasure. Many times the treasure has been sought for, but no bottom could be found to the stone; and hence it was supposed to be protected by the devil. Still adventurers continued to dig, until the excavated hollow round the base of the stone became filled with water, and it stood in the

centre of a small lake. Then an attempt was made to draw it out of its place by a yoke of oxen, who strained so hard at the task that the chains snapped, and the attempt proved abortive; although the guardian spirit of the stone appears to have taken alarm at the project, for he is said to have flown away in the shape of a drake, at the moment when the chains broke. Subsequently the stone sank into the earth, and totally disappeared, and for many years the plough passed over it.

In all material points, I am persuaded that this tradition is purely mythological; for the Drake Stone was but slightly fixed in the earth, and at the time when these attempts were said to have been made, the bottom could not have exceeded a foot and a half from the surface of the ground; besides which, no one pretends to assert that any of these experiments occurred in his time; and the oldest person I have consulted, says, that 'he had the tale from his fore-elders'.

Whatever the truth of the above account, Ethel Rudkin recorded the moving of the stone (actually there were two stones but they were referred to as one), under the instruction of the local vicar, Revd William Dodsworth, in about 1920, from higher ground two fields away from the church (in a north-westerly direction). A traction engine was used to help with the task and photographs taken of the occasion.

2

OF FOOLS
AND FARMING

In this section I have included six tales about characters within
the rural landscape. The linking of fools with farming should
not be seen as devaluing the important role that farmers had,
and continue to have, in food and other crop production.
The first tale is a traditional humorous story of the Lad that
went to look for Fools, which was collected by Mabel Peacock;
the second, Fred the Fool is taken from the collection of
Legends of the Carrs and is a reworking to unite the two halves
of what were obviously the same tale. This is followed by two
more tales collected by Marie Balfour about fools (or perhaps
the same Fool as they were told by the same person!)

The section ends with two short
fables again from Mabel Peacock,
The Fox and the House Dog
and The Fox in the Horse-Stable,
both of which are set within the
rural Lincolnshire landscape.

THE LAD THAT WENT TO LOOK FOR FOOLS

Once, when I was sitting in front of the Pywipe, down by the river at Lincoln, a man came up with one of them there barges and sits himself down, and after a bit we gets to talking and had a pot of beer together. He was from out of Oxfordshire, and he told me a rum tale about folks that lived in them parts, and said it was all as true as the Bible; but I tend to think that he'd put a bit or two to it himself, to top it up like. Well, he told me that there was an old man and his wife, and they had got a nice bit of land of their own and a nice bit of money in the bank as well. And they had just one child, a daughter, and the girl had a sweetheart that was called Jack.

One day, the old man was in the garden digging potatoes and he thinks to himself, 'If I haven't lived here five and thirty years, and never put no fencing round the well! Why, if our Polly marries Jack, and has a baby, it's certain to get into the water and drown itself!'

Then he sits down and starts crying and groaning, and out comes his wife and asks him what ails him. 'Why,' says he, 'if our Polly weds Jack, and has a bairn, it's bound to fall down the well and get drowned.'

'Aye, that's certain', says the old woman, and down she sits and begins sobbing and going on fit to kill herself.

Then out comes the lass as well, and asks, 'Whatever's the matter now? Has anything happened to Jack?'

'Nay,' says the old man, 'it's just that the well isn't fenced off, and if you and Jack gets married and has a bairn, it's sure to fall into the water and drown itself.'

'I never thought of that before,' says the lass, 'but it's true', and she was soon began crying as well.

And there they were bawling and carrying on, till they had almost wept enough to fill a washtub brimful of water. Well, it happened that Jack came up the lane and found them crying like young children. And he asked them if the cow had died in calving.

'Nay,' said the old man, 'it isn't that.'

'The bank hasn't broken with your money, has it?' says Jack.

'No,' says the old woman, 'it's not that.'

'Well then,' says Jack, 'what's up with you all?'

And they told him that it was the open well without a cage round it, and that if he weds Polly and she has a bairn, it's sure to fall into the water and get drowned. Well, when he heard that they was making all this to-do about nothing, he got as mad as a bear and said, 'I'll stop it from drowning, I won't get married at all, if supposing I can't find three folks that are as big a fools as you, before I've got a pair of new boots worn out.'

Then he slams the garden gate with a bang, goes to the shop and buys himself a pair of new boots, cuts himself an ash stick, to notch down all the fools he finds, and starts off to look for the most foolish folks he can find in all the countryside. Well, before long he came to a stackyard and saw a man busy shovelling something up against the stacks, but there was nowt at all in the shovel, and so Jack asked him what he reckoned he's doing.

And the man says, 'I'm shovelling sunshine up to dry the corn as it was gathered when it was too wet, but I don't seem to be getting anywhere with it.'

'Well, if ever I have seen a born fool, it's him,' says Jack. 'Why don't you set the sheaves up in stacks in the sun? They'd dry fast enough then.'

'I never thought of that before,' says the man. 'But however, I'll try it now', and he flings down the shovel, fetches his ladder, an' begins to tear the stack top off.

And Jack cuts a mark on his stick and walks a bit further. Before he'd gone very far he came upon a man that was trying to break a cobblestone open with his knife. 'What are you doing?' asked Jack.

'Why,' said the man, 'I want to get the kernel out of this stone, but the knife's so blunt that it slips and slithers instead of going in.'

'Here's another one of them', thinks Jack, and notches his ash stick again, and then he says to the man, 'You must get a hammer and break the cobble, if you want to know what's inside of it.'

'By God!' says the man. 'That thought never came into my head, but I'll see what I can do now.'

Well, Jack went a bit further and before long he came to an old thatched barn that was grown over with grass, and he saw a man sitting upon the ridge, trying to pull a cow up to the top of the barn by a band round its neck. He asked the man what he was doing, and the man said, 'There's a lot of grass up here, and I hate to see it wasted; but I can't get the cow up to eat it – she's that stupid, the more I pull one way the more she pulls the other.'

'This caps it all', thinks Jack, and he cuts another nick in his stick and says, 'Get your hook, you fool, and cut the grass of the thatch, and throw it down to the cow, then she'll eat it fast enough.'

'Lord save me!' says the man. 'If I'd been told to do that before, I wouldn't have choked so many cows with this here band,' and he goes off to look for his hook.

But Jack begins to think that Polly and her father and mother are no more stupid than folks are generally, and so he goes back and is married before he's got a month's wear out of his new boots.

Mabel Peacock included this story in her *Tales and Rhymes in Lindsey Folk-Speech*. The narrator referred to collecting the story from a bargee who had come from Oxfordshire, but the content of the story – the fear of drowning – is very suited to Lincolnshire. The narrator also mentions hearing the story in front of the Pyewipe Inn.

The tale is a variant of 'The Three Sillies', a traditional tale that has been found in Essex, Shropshire, Devonshire, Oxfordshire, and many other places. However, this particular version, with the emphasis on the fear of drowning in the well, is more like the Devonshire version as noted by Katharine Briggs, than that recorded by Vincent Sternberg in Oxfordshire, which has a more traditional core plot but does include an old woman trying to capture the sunshine to dry her corn.

FRED THE FOOL

There once was a lad named Fred Baddeley who took service with a farmer on the other side of the Wolds, and he came to a very bad end, he did. Well Fred was a foolish young man, and he was always getting in a mess with something or other, and he was the most awful lad to feed as ever there'd been anywhere. Sides of bacon, sacks of potatoes and loaves of bread – he'd swallow them down as if he had a bottomless pit instead of a stomach. Yet he was a thin, small slip of a lad, and looked as if he never ate nowt.

Well, a farmer saw him at the hirings and said, 'There's a chap that will not cost much to keep! He'll never eat the larder bare, not he – he's got no room for a store of food! Where you going lad?'

'Where you'll take me,' says Fred, for the farmers of Cliff way would have nothing to do with him, what with his eating and his foolish ways.

'I guess you aren't worth a wage,' says the farmer, with an eye to getting a bargain.

'I reckon I'm not much,' says the lad, for he was used to being told that.

'Well you are a fool,' says the farmer, scratching his head, 'telling me that! I shan't give you any wages. Will you come for the keep?'

'That I will,' says Fred, picking up, 'if you'll keep me in food and clothes.'

'I'll do that,' says the farmer, calculating that old clothes and house bits would keep him going. But he knew nowt about Fred!

It wasn't long before he found out that he'd made a strange bargain. He'd counted his cattle with a pair of calves to every heifer, as the saying goes, for Fred ate the house bare, and then swore he was still hungry.

And it was no use beating him, it only made him worse, as he'd eat more than ever afterwards, though the master thought that he'd be done for.

'Well!' says Fred to himself. 'Here I am, starving with hunger. I've not had a bite since morning, nowt but a bucket of potatoes and a cake of bread, or maybe two, and I am quite empty. The master said that he'd keep me in food, so I guess I'll go and try the storehouse. There's a side of bacon there, and maybe beef. The windows are barred, but I'm thin, so I'll probably get through.'

So off he went. But as soon as he got his head and shoulders between the bars, he stuck fast, and couldn't go back nor forwards! Well, instead of waiting and thinking of something that would get him out, he screeched out, as if he were being murdered, until the master himself came and found him half in, and the bigger half out, of the storehouse window!

'What are you doing there, damn you?' roared the farmer. 'Come out of there I tell you!'

'God almighty, if I could have got out, I could have got in too!' says Fred angry too. 'Can't you see that I'm stuck?'

'And what were you doing then, you fool?' screeched the master.

'I came to get something to eat, of course,' said the lad, kicking about all the time with his hind legs, 'the mistress was busy.'

'Busy, you say?' yelled the farmer. 'You are a thief, and I'll teach you to steal my meat!'

And up with his stick he began to beat him with all his might. And Fred had exposed a fine place for the beating to fall on. But by and by, along came the mistress who squealed out, 'Stop! If you beat him, he'll eat us out of house and home.'

'That's so!' said the farmer, and he thought for a bit. 'Well, I reckon I'll make him remember that I caught him stealing anyway!' said he, and pulled the nail from Fred's thumb.

Fred was glad to get free, and he didn't seem to fret about his nail. But by and by, he found his clothes had become rags and he could barely hold them together to hide his skin. 'A man must be decent, I guess,' says he to himself. 'They'll never let me go naked, I reckon. The master said he'd keep me in clothes, and he's got heaps of his own, so I'll go and get something to wear.'

And off he went to the house and took the farmer's new breeches and best coat, but they were so big he had to hold them up with two hands. But just as he got to the door, the master and his wife caught him again. 'What have you got there?' screeched the missus. 'My master's best clothes. Well I never! What will you do next? You are the biggest fool.'

'Damn you, you thief!' yells the farmer, red with anger and bristling like a hedgehog, 'I'll kick you till you're as black as rotten turnips, I will!'

'No!' cried his wife. 'He'll eat all my bacon if you do!'

But with his wife hanging on his arm, and blind with rage, the master picked up his axe with his other hand and struck at Fred, cutting off his hand at the wrist bone. Fred howled.

'Well I didn't plan to do it!' says the farmer, a bit afraid, 'but if you tell folk that I have done it, I will call the police and get you up for thieving!'

But bless him! Fred was such a fool. He had no idea that he could have had the master done for it, and he took the beating. And he went to the doctor, but nothing could be done to save his hand. You would think he would have gone away then. But he didn't, poor fool! He said, 'Oh, I've lost my hand and my nail before that, and I've got kind of used to it, so I reckon I'll stay with the farmer.'

Well, it happened that the farmer was strange and disliked in the countryside, and he'd heard it said that one day he would get up in the morning and find his ricks burnt, and he was getting scared of this. So every night, one of the hands would keep watch in the yard until dawn.

Soon as Fred was out of the doctor's hands, the master told him to do the watching as he wasn't much good in the fields. 'I'll do it,' said Fred, 'if you let me sleep in the day.'

But no, the master wouldn't do that. He must run errands all day and do light jobs. He must earn his keep *and* watch all night, or he'd turn him out.

'Well, here's to trying!' said Fred. 'And the Lord keep them off the ricks if I go to sleep!'

The first night or two he stayed awake most of the time, but afterwards he took to sleeping as if he was in his bed. And naturally, at last, it came as expected – the farmer was woken up by a bright light, and as soon as he looked out of the window, there were his ricks all blazing. Down he went in his bare legs, raging and swearing. 'Where's the scoundrel?' he yelled.

And he saw Fred, sleeping sound as a baby in the muck beside the pigs in the yard. The farmer said nothing, but he looked like a white devil, shining with evil and spite, and he walked over and picked up the lad and dragged him to the blazing ricks. And before Fred realised what was happening, the farmer picked him up and heaved him into the middle of the blazing rick.

'Keep off!' he said, stuttering and stammering with anger. 'I'll kill anyone that lifts a hand to help him!' and he took hold of a great stone and stared. And the fellas were so afraid of him, that before they could decide what to do, Fred was burnt up in the middle of the rick, where he had got caught in the ropes and couldn't get loose.

Anyway, after a while ,Fred's spirit got up and thought about what he must do next. And something said to him, 'You must go down below the earth and tell the Great Worm that you're dead, and ask him to get you eaten up, or you'll never rest.'

'Well I'm willing,' said Fred. And off he went, asking his way and rubbing shoulders with all horrid things glowering round about him.

He came to a great place where it was dark, with glimmering lights crossing it, and full of an earthy smell, with whiffs of awful stink as would turn your stomach.

And underfoot were creeping things, and all around were crawling, fluttering things, and the air was hot and mucky.

At the end of the place was a horrid great worm, coiled up on a flat stone, with his slimy head moving and swinging from side to side as if it was smelling for its dinner.

The worm shot out his horrid head right in Fred's face and said, 'Are you, Fred? So you're dead and buried, and food for the worms, are you? Well, where's your body?'

'Please, your worship,' said Fred, not wanting to annoy him, naturally. 'I'm all here.'

'No,' said the worm, 'do you think that we can eat you? You are dead my lad; you must find your body, if you want to rest in the mools.'

'But where is it? My body?' said Fred, scratching his head.

'Where is it buried?' said the worm.

'It isn't buried; that's just it!' said Fred. 'It's ashes; I was burnt up.'

'Oh!' said the worm. 'That's bad; you'll not taste good. Don't fret; go for the ashes, and bring them here, and we'll do all we can.'

Well, Fred went back, and he looked and looked, and he got all the ashes together that he could see and took them off in a sack to the Great Worm. He opened the sack, and the worm crawled down and he smelt him and turned him over and over.

'Fred,' he said, 'something's missing. You're not all here, Fred. Where's the rest of you?'

'I've brought all I could find,' said Fred, shaking his head.

'Nay!' said the worm. 'There's a hand missing.'

'Ooh! That's so!' said Fred, nodding. 'I'd lost the hand I had: cut off, it was.'

'You must find it Fred.'

'Well, I've no idea where the doctor put it, but I'll go and see.'

So off he went again, and looked here and looked there, and he got it. Back he went to the worm. 'Here's the hand,' says Fred.

And the worm turned it over. 'No, there's something still missing, Fred,' says he. 'Have you lost anything else?'

'Let me see,' says Fred, thinking. 'I'd lost a nail, and it never grew again.'

'That's it, I reckon,' says the worm. 'You've got to find it, Fred.'

'I reckon I'll never find that, then, master,' says Fred, 'but I'm willing to try.' And off he went. But a nail is an easy thing to lose, and a hard thing to find, and though he sought and sought he couldn't find it. And so he went back to the worm.

'I've sought and I've sought, and I've found nothing,' says he. 'Can't you make do without it?'

'No!' said the worm, 'I can't – are you certain you can't find it, Fred?'

'Certain, worse luck!'

'You must walk the earth until you do find it then!'

'But what if I can never find it?'

'Then you must walk all the time! I'm sorry for this, Fred, but you'll have lots o' company!'

And all the creeping things and the crawling things took and turned Fred about; and ever since, if he's not found his nail, he's walking about seeking for it.

The previous tale was collected in two separate parts by Marie Balfour, though she acknowledged that they seemed to be connected. The first 'half', called Fred the Fool, was collected from a man who lived in the Wolds. Marie met the man whilst she had to spend an hour in a North Lincolnshire Inn, some distance from her home in Redbourne. The second 'half' was told to her by Fanny, the young girl who narrated the story of the Dead Moon. The girl called the main character in her tale Samuel, and Marie gave the tale the name Sam'l's Ghost, but I have opted to use the name Fred for the combined tale.

The tale reflects a number of aspects of life in rural Lincolnshire including the practice of hiring workers who would 'live in' at the farm; the fear of arson attacks as mechanisation took hold; the belief that there was a 'Great Worm' that lived beneath the earth, and the belief that a body should be buried whole. The tale also contains parallels with a Lincolnshire coast story of a smuggler who, when caught, was sentenced to have his right hand chopped off. The punishment did not stop him and the next time he was caught he was ordered to pay a fine of six pounds (the equivalent of six years' work), which soon put a halt to his smuggling activities.

Coat o' Clay

Once upon a time, in the parts of Lindsey, there lived a wise woman. Some said she was a witch, but they said it in a whisper, lest she should overhear and do them a mischief. And truly it was not a thing one could be sure of, for she was never known to hurt anyone, which, if she were a witch, she would have been sure to do. But she could tell you what your sickness was and how to cure it with herbs, and she could mix rare potions that would drive the pain out of you in a twinkling; and she could advise you what to do if your cows were ill, or if you'd got into trouble, and tell the maids whether their sweethearts were likely to be faithful.

But she was not best pleased if folks questioned her too much or too long, and she disliked fools. Many came to her asking foolish things, as was their nature, and to them she never gave counsel, at least of a kind that could aid them much.

One day, as she sat at her door paring potatoes, over the stile and up the path came a tall lad with a long nose and goggle eyes, and his hands in his pockets.

'That's a fool if ever was one, and a fool's luck in his face,' said the wise woman to herself with a nod of her head, and threw a potato skin over her left shoulder to keep off ill-chance.

'Good day, missus,' said the fool. 'I be come to see thee.'

'So thou be,' said the wise woman. 'I see that. How's all in thy folk this year?'

'Oh, they're fair,' answered he. 'But they say I be a fool.'

'Ay, so thou be,' nodded she, and threw away a bad potato. 'I see that too. But what do you want o' me? I keep no brains for sale.'

'Well, see now. Mother says I'll ne'er be wiser all my born days; but folk tell as thou canst do everything. Can't thee learn me a bit, so they'll think me a clever fellow at home?'

'Hout-tout!' said the wise woman. 'Thou art a bigger fool than I thought. Nay, I can't learn thee nought, lad, but I can tell thee su mmat. Thou'll be a fool all thy days till thou gets a coat o' clay, and then thou'll know more 'n me.'

'Hi, missus, what sort of a coat's that?' said he.

'That's none o' my business,' answered she. 'Thou'st got to find out that.'

And she took up her potatoes and went into her house.

The fool took off his cap and scratched his head. 'It's a queer kind of a coat to look for, sure-ly,' said he. 'I never heard on a coat o' clay. But then I be a fool, that's true.'

So he walked on till he came to the drain nearby, with just a trickle of watter and a foot of mud in it.

'Here's muck,' said the fool, much pleased, and he got in and rolled in it and came out spluttering. 'Hi yi,' said he – for he had his mouth full – 'I've got a coat o' clay now to be sure. I'll go home and tell my mother I'm a wise man and not a fool any longer.' And he went on home.

Presently, he came to a cottage with a ramping lass at the door.

'Morning, fool,' said she, 'hast thou been ducked in the horse-pond?'

'Fool yourself,' said he, 'the wise woman says I'll know more 'n she when I get a coat o' clay, and here it is. Shall I marry thee, lass?'

'Ay,' said she, for she thought she'd like a fool for a husband, 'when shall it be?'

'I'll come and fetch thee when I've told my mother,' said the fool, and he gave her his lucky penny and went on.

When he got home his mother was on the doorstep.

'Mother, I've got a coat o' clay,' said he.

'Coat o' muck,' said she, 'an' what o' that?'

'Wise woman said I'd know more'n she when I got a coat o' clay,' said he, 'so I down in the drain an' got one, an' I'm not a fool any longer.'

'Very good,' said his mother, 'now thou can get a wife.'

'Ay,' said he, 'I'm going to marry so-an'-so.'

'What?!' said his mother. 'That lass? No, that thou'll not. She's nought but a brat, wi' ne'er a cow or a cabbage o' her own, an' bears a bad name into the bargain.'

'But I gave her my luck-penny,' said the fool.

'Then thou art a bigger fool than ever, for all thy coat o' clay!' said his mother, and banged the door in his face.

'Dang it!' said the fool, and scratched his head, 'that's not the right sort o' clay, sure-ly.'

So back he went to the high road and sat down on the bank of the river close by, looking at the water, which was cool and clear.

By and by he fell asleep, and before he knew what he was about, he rolled off into the river with a splash, and scrambled out, dripping like a drowned rat.

'Dear, dear,' said he, 'I'd better go and get dry in the sun.' So up he went to the high road and lay down in the dust, rolling about so that the sun should get at him all over.

Presently, when he sat up and looked down at himself he found that the dust had caked into a sort of skin over his wet clothes till you could not see an inch of them they were so well covered. 'Hi, yi!' said he. 'Here's a coat o' clay ready made, an' a fine one. See now, I'm a clever fellow this time sure-ly, for I've found what I wanted wi'out lookin' for it! Wow, but it's a fine feeling to be so smart!'

And he sat and scratched his head, and thought about his own cleverness.

But all of a sudden, round the corner came the squire on horseback, full gallop, as if the bogles were after him; but the fool had to jump, even though the squire pulled his horse back on his haunches.

'What the dickins,' said the squire, 'do you mean by lying in the middle of the road like that?'

'Well, master,' said the fool, 'I fell into the water and got wet, so I lay down in the road to get dry; an' I lay down a fool an' got up a wise man.'

'How's that?' said the squire.

So the fool told him about the wise woman and the coat o' clay.

'Ha, ha!' laughed the squire. 'Whoever heard of a wise man lying in the middle of the high road to be ridden over. Lad, take my word for it, you're a bigger fool than ever,' and he rode on laughing.

'Dang it!' said the fool as he scratched his head. 'I've not got the right sort of coat yet then.' And he choked and spluttered in the dust that the squire's horse had raised.

So, on he went in a melancholy mood till he came to an inn, the landlord standing at his door smoking.

'Well, fool,' said he, 'thou art fine an' mucky.'

'Ay,' said the fool, 'I be mucky outside an' dusty in, but it's not the right thing yet.'

And he told the landlord all about the wise woman and the coat o' clay.

'Hout-tout!' said the landlord with a wink. 'I know what's wrong. Thou'st got a skin of muck outside an' all dry dust inside. Thou must moisten it, lad, wi' a good drink, an' then thou'll ha' real all-over coat o' clay.'

'Hi,' said the fool, 'that's a good word.'

So down he sat and began to drink. But it was wonderful how much liquor it took to moisten so much dust, and each time he got to the bottom of the glass he found he was still dry. At last he began to feel very merry and pleased with himself.

'Hi, yi!' said he. 'I've got a real coat o' clay now outside and in – what a difference it do make to be sure. I feel another man now – so smart!'

And he told the landlord he was certainly a wise man now, though he couldn't speak over-distinctly after drinking so much. So up he got, and thought he would go home and tell his mother she hadn't a fool for a son any more. But just as he was trying to get through the inn door, which would scarcely keep still long enough for him to find it, up came the landlord and caught him by the sleeve.

'See here, master,' said he. 'Thou hasn't paid thy score – where's my money?'

'Haven't any!' said the fool, and pulled out his pockets to show they were empty.

'What?!' said the landlord, and swore. 'Thou'st drunk all my liquor and ha'nt got nought to pay for it?'

'Ay!' said the fool. 'You told me to drink so as to get a coat o' clay; but as I'm a wise man now I don't mind helping thee along in the world a bit, for though I'm a smart fellow I'm not too proud to my friends.'

'Wise man! Smart fellow!' said the landlord, 'An' help me along, wilt tha'! Dang it! Thou art the biggest fool I've ever seen, an' it's I'll help thee first – out o' this!' And he kicked him out of the door into the road, and swore at him.

'Hum,' said the fool as he lay in the dust. 'I'm not so wise as I thought. I guess I'll go back to the wise woman and tell her there's a screw loose somewhere.'

So up he got and went along to her house, and found her sitting at the door.

'So thou'st come back,' said she, with a nod. 'What dost thou want wi' me now?'

So he sat down and told her how he'd tried to get a coat o' clay, but he wasn't any wiser for all of it.

'No,' said the wise woman, 'thou art a bigger fool than ever, my lad.'

'So they all say,' sighed the fool, 'but where can I get the right sort of coat o' clay, then, missus?'

'When thou'st done wi' this world, an' thy fo'ak put thee in the ground,' said the wise woman. 'That's the only coat o' clay 'at'll make such as thee wise, lad. Born a fool, die a fool, an' be a fool thy life long, an' that's the truth!'

And she went into the house and shut the door.

'Dang it!' said the fool. 'I must tell my mother she was right after all, an' that she'll niver ha' a wise man for a son!'

And he went off home.

Marie Balfour described this tale as a 'droll', and indeed it is whimsically humorous. She also revealed that it was collected from the same person who gave her the next tale,

'A Pottle of Brains'. However, she did not give their name or any clues to their identity.

The tale has some interesting aspects and, as well as being explicitly set in Lindsey, it also contains references to drains (rivers), the high road (which is often called the Ramper) and bogles (ghosts). Some particularly interesting expressions are 'screw loose', which was recorded from 1810 as referring to mental weakness; 'lucky penny', which refers to the money returned for luck by a seller of an item, and 'what the dickins' which is a reference to the 'Devil' or 'Devilkin' (shortened to dickins). The latter was included by William Shakespeare in *The Merry Wives of Windsor*.

A POTTLE OF BRAINS

There was once a fool that wanted to buy a pottle o' brains, for he was forever getting into scrapes through his foolishness and being laughed at by everyone. Folk told him that he could get everything he liked from the wise woman that lived on top of the hill, and dealt in potions and herbs and spells and things, and could tell you all that would come to you and your folk. So he told his mother, and asked her if he should see the wise woman and buy a pottle of brains.

'That you should,' said she, 'you've sore need of them, my son; and if I should die, who'd take care of a poor fool such as you, no more fit to look after yourself than an unborn baby? But mind your manners and speak to her politely my lad, for the wise folk are easily mis-pleased.'

So off he went after his tea, and there she was, sitting by the fire, and stirring a big pot.

'Good evening missus,' says he, 'it's a fine night.'

'Aye,' says she, and went on stirring.

'It might rain,' says he, and fidgeted from one foot to the other.

'Maybe,' says she.

'And maybe it won't,' says he, and looked out of the window.

'Perhaps,' says she.

And he scratched his head and twisted his hat. 'Well,' says he, 'I can't remember anything else about the weather, but let me see; the crops are getting on fine.'

'Fine,' says she.

'And the beasts are fattening,' says he.

'They are,' says she.

'And – and –' says he, and comes to a stop. 'I reckon we'll tackle the business now, having done the polite part. Have you any brains for sale?'

'That depends,' says she, 'if you want king's brains or soldier's brains or schoolmaster's brains – I do not keep them.'

'No,' says he, 'just ordinary brains – fit for any fool – same as everyone has about here; something common like.'

'Ah, yes,' says the wise woman, 'I might manage that, if you'll help yourself.'

'How is that missus?' says he.

'Just so,' says she, looking in her pot. 'Bring me the heart of the thing you like best of all, and I'll tell you where to get your pottle of brains.'

'But,' says he, scratching his head, 'how can I do that?'

'That's not for me to say,' says she, 'find out for yourself my lad, if you don't want to be a fool all of your days! But you'll have to read me a riddle so I can see you've brought the right thing, and if your brains are about you. And I've something else to see to,' says she, 'so good evening to you.' And with that she carried the pot away with her into the back place.

So off goes the fool to his mother, to tell her what the wise woman said. 'And I reckon I'll have to kill that pig,' says he, 'for I like bacon better than everything.'

'Then do it, my lad,' said his mother, 'for certain it will all be a strange and good thing for you, if you can buy a pottle of brains, and be able to look after your own self.'

So he killed the pig and next day off he went to the wise woman's cottage, and there she sat, reading a great book. 'Good evening, missus,' says he, 'I've brought you the heart of the thing I like best of all.'

'Ah yes?' says she, and looked at him through her spectacles. 'Tell me this then, what runs without feet?'

He scratched his head, and thought, and thought, but he couldn't tell.

'Go away,' says she, 'you've not got me the right thing yet. I've no brains for you today.' And she clapped the book together and turned her back on him.

So off the fool went to tell his mother. But as he got near the house, out came folk running to tell him that his mother was dying. And when he got in, his mother looked at him and smiled, as if to say she could leave him with a quiet mind, since he'd got brains enough now to look after himself – and then she died. So down he sat, and the more he thought about it the worse he felt. He remembered how she had nursed him when he was a tiddy brat and helped him with his lessons, and cooked his dinners, and mended his clothes, and put up with his foolishness; and he felt sorrier and sorrier, and began to sob and cry.

'Oh mother, mother!' says he, 'who'll take care of me now! You shouldn't have left me alone, for I liked you better than everything!'

And as he said that, he thought of the words of the wise woman. 'Hi, yi!' says he, 'must I cut out my mother's heart and take it to her?' and he took out a knife and felt the edge.

'No! I can't do it,' says he. 'What will I do? What will I do to get that pottle o' brains, now I am alone in the world?' So he thought, and thought, and the next day he went and borrowed a sack and bundled his mother in, and carried it on his shoulder up to the wise woman's cottage.

'Good evening, missus,' says he, 'I reckon I've got the right thing this time surely,' and he dropped the sack down – kerflap! – on the doorsill.

'Maybe,' says the wise woman, 'but read me this, now, what's yellow and shining but isn't gold?'

And he scratched his head, and thought, and thought, but he couldn't tell.

'You've not brought the right thing my lad,' says she. 'You're a bigger fool than I thought!' and shut the door in his face.

He sat down by the roadside and cried. 'I've lost the only two things that I cared for, and what else can I find to buy a pottle of brains with!' he thought, and he howled until the tears ran down into his mouth. And up came a lass who lived nearby, and she looked at him.

'What's up with you fool?' says she.

'Oh, I've killed my pig, and lost my mother, and I am nothing but a fool myself,' says he, sobbing.

'That's bad,' says she, 'and have you nobody to look after you?'

'Naw,' says he, 'and I can't buy my pottle of brains for there's nothing I like best left!'

'What are you talking about?' says she.

And down she sits by him, and he told her all about the wise woman and the pig, and his mother and the riddles, and that he is alone in the world. 'Well,' says she, 'I wouldn't mind looking after you myself.'

'Could you do it?' says he.

'Oh yes!' says she, 'folk says that fools make good husbands, and I reckon I'll have thee, if you're willing.'

'Can you cook?' says he.

'Yes, I can,' says she.

'And scrub?' says he.

'Surely,' says she.

'And mend my clothes?' says he.

'I can that,' says she.

'I reckon you'll do then as well as anybody,' says he. 'But, what will I do about this wise woman?'

'Oh, wait a bit,' says she, 'something might turn up, and it will not matter if you are a fool, as long as you've got me to look after you.'

'That's true,' says he, and off they went and got married. And she kept his house so clean and neat, and cooked his dinner so fine, that one night he says to her, 'Lass, I'm thinking I like you best of everything, after all.'

'That's good to hear,' says she 'and what then?'

'Have I got to kill you, do you think, and take your heart up to the wise woman for that pottle of brains?'

'Lord, no!' says she, looking scared. 'I wouldn't have that. But see here; you didn't cut out your mother's heart did you?'

'No, but if I had, maybe I'd have got my pottle of brains,' says he.

'Not a bit of it,' says she. 'Just you take me as I am, heart and all, and I wager I will help you read the riddles.'

'Can you do this?' says he, doubtful like. 'I reckon they're too hard for women-folk'

'Well,' says she, 'let's see now. Tell me the first one.'

'What runs without feet?' says he.

'Why water!' says she.

'It does,' says he, and scratched his head. 'And what's yellow and shining, but isn't gold?'

'Why, the sun!' says she.

'Why yes, it is!' says he. 'Come, we'll go up to the wise woman at once,' and off they went. And as they came up the path, she was sitting at the door, plaiting straws.

'Good evening, missus,' says he.

'Good evening, fool,' says she.

'I reckon that I have found the right thing at last,' says he, 'though I haven't exactly cut the heart out, it is such mucky work.'

The wise woman looked at them both and wiped her spectacles. 'Can you tell me what has first no legs, and then two legs, and ends with four legs?'

And the fool scratched his head, and thought, and thought, but he couldn't tell. And the lass whispered in his ear, 'It would be a tadpole.'

'Perhaps,' says he, then, 'it might be a tadpole, missus.'

The wise woman nodded her head. 'That's right,' says she, 'and you've got your pottle of brains already.'

'Where are they?' says he, looking about, and feeling in his pockets.

'In your wife's head,' says she. 'The only cure for a fool is a good wife to look after him, and that you've got; so good evening to you!' And with that she nodded to them, and got up and went into the house.

So they went home together, and he never wanted to buy a pottle of brains again, for his wife had enough for the both of them.

Mabel Peacock acknowledged that she had worked the following two fables 'to the local speech of Lindsey' for inclusion in her *Taales fra Linkisheere*. She does not say whether she had heard them locally, but as she included local places within the narratives, I have included them within this book.

THE FOX AND THE HOUSE DOG

Old Reynold the fox came out one bitterly cold night to see if he could find something to clean his teeth on and fill his belly with. He was that hungry, he was half dead, and as he crept along the hedge bottom he said to himself, 'If I don't find a rabbit pretty quick, I shall die. Rabbits should be out gnarling at thorns and things in frost like this, but it is plain enough to see that they have no thought for other folk, they lie snug and warm in their burrows, when their betters are hunting for food in the snow and wind. Maybe I should slip over to Sawcliffe and see if I can find anything there. Them young stags, newly born, should be a fair picking.'

And he shoots off down the lane as quick as he can lift his feet off the ground, for he'd been living on carrion and strays ever since the snow first came, and he felt as if he had nothing in his insides from Mayday to Martlemass.

But when he got to Sawcliffe farm and was just turning into the yard, he ran straight into the yard dog.

'Hello,' said the dog, 'what's brought you here?'

'Why,' said the fox, cheekily, 'chickens have brought me, if you must know. Meat is strange and hard to get in these bad times, and I'm driven to taking the handiest thing I can find; and I expect that handiest thing tonight will be something out of yonder fowl house of yours.'

The dog replied, 'Bad times! If you were in service you wouldn't know about bad times, I have my fill of meat and a good fire to lie by as well, as long as I look after the house and keep the tramps away from the yard.'

'Aye,' said the fox, looking at the dog out of the corner of his eye, 'you're as fat as a fifty-stone pig and your coat shines like sun glinting upon the new canal at low water; but just tell me one thing, what's this strap for, that is buckled round your neck?'

'Strap,' said the dog, 'that's nothing, at least it is as good as nowt. It is just for when they want to chain me up, you know.'

'Chain,' said the fox, 'then those that are in service have to stay where other folk like to put them, is that it? None of that for me. I come when I like, and go when I like, and wherever I like; and neither with your leave, or by your leave either. Meat and drink is a bit too dear when folk has to wear chains to buy them.'

THE FOX IN THE HORSE STABLE

One day, when hunters were after Reynold the Fox and he was so tired he could run no further, he bolted into a stack-yard, ran up a ladder that was leaning against a haystack, jumped from the haystack onto the wagon-shade, slid down the other side, then slipped through the stable door and hid himself in the straw under the crib.

'Well, you are a fool,' said the black mare, 'if ever there was one. The men will be back for their dinner by now, and they are bound to see you.'

'Don't tire yourself,' said Reynold the Fox, snuggling down and listening to see if the foxhounds had found out where he was hiding. 'I'm sure the lads will never give me a thought. I know what chaps are; their heads are overfull of sweethearts and such stuff for anything else to get in.'

'Well, but the bailiff will see you,' said the mare, 'that's for sure. He's sure to come round to take a look at things before long.'

'Let him come for all I care,' said the fox. 'He'll be busy thinking of the twenty-stone pig that he fattened when his master was bed-bound with rheumatics and couldn't keep account of potatoes and meal to think of me. I'm not going to scare myself with anything, least of all about him.'

After a while, the waggoner and the bailiff came in and did not notice the fox, and went out again. But before long, the master himself took a look around the yard; and he was barely over the threshold when he saw the fox's tail peeping out of the straw. He called the waggoner and said, 'What's that under the crib in the black mare's stall? It almost looks like a polecat.'

And then he snatched up the muck-fork that was in the corner near the corn bin, and was just about to knock the polecat on the head when up jumped the fox, who ran away out the door between the wheat stacks and over the fence in a jiffy, singing out as he ran, 'If master does as master should do, one of his head's worth bailiff's two'.

3

OF STRANGE
CREATURES

This chapter will look at tales of creatures that are not human, commencing with a tale collected by Ruth Tongue from her family in Alkborough: 'The Man in the Wilderness'. The story was included within the collection *Folktales of England*, and I have adapted some of the language used within the narrative to include terms used in the area. The tale is about a wild man living in a wood who will only let people pass if they can solve a riddle. The second tale is also about a man in a wood, but this one seems to be a tale composed to make sense of the presence of some strange artefacts within the parish church at Stainfield.

The third tale included here is taken from Tongue's 1970 collection *Forgotten Folktales of the English Counties* and also contains riddles. But instead of a wild man, the main characters are a giant and a dwarf, the latter of which I have changed to a boggart, being the Lincolnshire term for a small kind of fairy creature. The tale also seeks to explain the origins of the Lincoln Cliff as a means of protecting Gainsborough.

It is followed by an exploration of a number of tales about a malevolent little creature known as a hob, hob-thrush or hob-thrust that haunts a farm at East Halton. The final tale is a traditional tale collected by Mabel Peacock about how a farmer gets the better of a deal that he has made with a fairy creature.

THE MAN IN THE WILDERNESS

Tom, Dick and Little Jack were going to the fair when they came to a wood where a wild man lived that no one could get rid of. The creature was a big hairy man-like creature, and the boys knew that he would ask travellers a question, and if they couldn't tell the answer they were never seen again. So Tom said, 'I'm the eldest, so I'll go first.'

The other boys waited and by and by, Tom came back and said:

The man in the wilderness asked of me
How many blackberries grow in the sea?
I answered him, as I thought good,
As many as red herrings grow in the wood.

'And he had to let me go.'

So Dick then said, 'It's my turn next' and he went off to see the creature.

And the other boys waited and by and by, Dick came back and said:

> The man in the wilderness asked me
> Why his hen could swim and his pig could fly?
> I answered him briskly, as I thought best,
> Because they were born in a cuckoo's nest.

'And he had to let me go.'

Now it was young Jack's turn, and he said, 'I'll go now' and he went off to see the creature.

And the other boys waited, and all of a sudden there was a great puff of smoke, and by and by, Little Jack came back and said:

> The man in the wilderness asked me tell,
> The sands in the sea and I counted them well.
> Says he with a grin 'And not one more?'
> I answered him, bravely, 'You go and make sure!'

'So he had to go, and the wild man's now in the sea, and the sea will keep him.'

So Tom, Dick and Little Jack went to the fair quite safely.

'The Man in the Wilderness' was recorded by folklorist Katharine Briggs from Ruth Tongue on 28 September 1963. Ruth had heard it from her aunt, Annie Tongue of Alkborough, who said she had heard it from her grandmother in 1860, who had it from her mother in about 1800.

Katharine speculated on the origins of the story and whether it had been composed to enhance a popular nursery rhyme. Riddles and rhymes were popular in North Lincolnshire, and Mabel Peacock included thirty-eight riddles in *Tales and Rhymes in the Lindsey Folk-Speech,* and six tales that included short rhymes or couplets within *Taales fra Linkisheere.* Riddles also form a core part of 'A Pottle of Brains', collected by Marie Balfour.

'The Man in the Wilderness' could be influenced by the wild man stories, which centre on the village of Stainfield, West Lindsey, as outlined below, or similar wild men found at Orford in Suffolk or Salisbury in Wiltshire. He could also be compared to Lailoken, the semi-legendary prophet and madman who lived in the Caledonian Forest in the late sixth century, a character not dissimilar to Merlin.

Alkborough is a small village in North Lincolnshire, at the northern end of the Lincoln Cliff, overlooking the Humber Estuary at the Trent Falls, the confluence of the rivers Ouse and Trent. The village has been occupied since Neolithic times, and Mills, in his *Dictionary of English Place Names* (1998) translates the name as 'wood or grave of a man called Alca'. Close to the cliff edge is Julian's Bower, an ancient turf maze, or labyrinth.

THE WILD MAN OF STAINFIELD

It was once said that a ferocious wild man lived in the woods at Lissinglea, not far from Lissington. The man, who was semi-human and covered in hair, killed the animals in the wood and terrorised the people of the district.

A knight named Drake Tyrwhit was offered all the land of Stainfield, near Wragby, including 280 acres of woodland and land at Lissinglea, if he would kill the wild man. When Tyrwhit got to the woods he found the wild man asleep on a bank by a pit, with pyewipes (lapwings) flying

around him making a lot of noise to wake him so that he would not be killed, or to stop Tyrwhit from getting close. The knight rode up to the wild man, and from his horse used his sword to run him through as he lay on the ground. The wild man jumped up, streaming with blood, and chased Tyrwhit for a mile before he fell. The knight then turned his horse round again and used his sword to finish him off.

According to some, the blood stained the field around, giving the land its name. Others say that the name was derived from the Scandinavian *'stain'* (stony) and *'feld'* (field). Another version of the story, set in the twelfth century, describes the knight as being newly returned from the crusades, to find that he had been dispossessed of his estates and went to live in the woods.

A further variant of the story has the wild man killed, not by a knight, but by a band of local farmers who wanted to kill the man who was stealing their livestock and terrorising their families. After a fierce struggle, these farmers, collectively known as 'The Hardy Gang', trapped and killed the man in a wood between Langton and Stainfield, which is now known after them.

Other variations have Tyrwhit pouring a barrel of rum into the pond in the wood where the wild man lived and then killing him whilst he was too drunk to fight. Or Tyrwhit shooting the man whilst he was asleep then burying his body beneath a stone outside the church.

So, what might be the truth behind this tale?

Drake Tyrwhit's coat of arms had three pyewipes on it. His helm had a crest on top, decorated with a wild man, naked except for foliage around his waist, holding a club in his right hand. This seems more like a depiction of the wodewose, a creature from ancient myth, popular in medieval times and a symbol of strength, fertility and honour, than a local wild man.

It is known that the Tyrwhit family moved from Kettleby, a once thriving village near Bigby, to the hamlet of Stainfield in the sixteenth century, at the time of the Dissolution of the Monasteries, when they were rewarded by Henry VIII with the gift of Stainfield Priory and Bardney Abbey.

The knight's helm, including the crest, his jerkin, his dagger and his gloves, were put on display in the church for many years. Sadly the items, with the exception of the crest, were stolen from the church in 1995.

It was also believed that tattered and faded fabric that once hung in the church were the clothes once belonging to the wild man, but these were found to be banners embroidered by the ladies of the family depicting the Creed, the Lord's Prayer and the Ten Commandments. The remnants of the banners are now in the care of the County Archives in Lincoln.

IN MY POCKET

A giant and a boggart were good friends and always went everywhere together. The giant was big and stupid and the boggart was little and clever, so they worked very well as a team.

One day, when they were looking for something to eat, they saw some sheep.

'I could eat a little mutton,' said the boggart.

'I could eat a lot of mutton,' said the giant.

'But we must pay for it with work,' said the boggart, 'as we have no money. And we will only take one of the small sheep.'

The boggart called his brothers out of the hill. They were also hungry and they all took the little sheep and killed it, and were just about to eat it when they noticed that the giant had killed two fat rams. The brothers then saw the wizard who owned the land coming towards them and they ran back to the hill, while the little boggart jumped into the giant's pocket and hid. The giant was too stupid to run.

'Who has killed my ram with the golden horns?'

'Not me,' said the little boggart in the pocket with a big voice like the giant's.

'And who has killed my ram with the silver horns?'

'Not me,' said the little boggart in the pocket in the big voice.

'And who has killed my little curly coat lamb?'

'Not me,' squeaked the stupid giant, when the little boggart in his pocket gave him a pinch.

The wizard could not do anything about it because he could tell that he had been told the truth. So he said, 'We will have a riddling contest, and if I guess the answer to yours, you will serve me for one hundred years, and if I'm wrong and you guess mine, you may have all the sheep.'

The giant agreed to this, because the little boggart in his pocket told him to.

'Cold feet, cold head, brown, dry, not dead – what's that?' said the wizard.

The giant scratched his head, but the little boggart said in a big voice, 'A winter tree, master.' And he was right.

'You may have the sheep,' said the wizard, 'but I will win your service for a hundred years. Let's hear your riddle.'

The giant listened to the little boggart in his pocket and then said, very slowly, 'Two for one' (for the giant was twice as big as the wizard), 'A small one for the rest,' (for the boggart's brothers), 'And a little, little piece for my pocket,' (and that was the little boggart).

The wizard could not guess the answer and so he went away.

The brothers came back from the hill, and they and the little boggart went to look for the white curly coat lamb, but found that the giant had eaten him too. So they got another sheep and went off to eat it.

By and by, the wizard came back and found the giant still eating, but this time he had killed an ox.

'Who killed my fine black ox?' asked the wizard.

'Not me,' said the stupid giant, remembering what he had said before. But he had not told the truth and the wizard knew it, and so made the giant work for him for a hundred years.

They say that the giant had to dig up some of the hills in Yorkshire and carry them to Lincolnshire, where he was to put them all along the River Trent to keep the floods away from Gainsborough.

The story was also collected by Ruth Tongue, who specu-lated that it was a Norse tale from the oral tradition and wondered if it was familiar to Professor J.R.R. Tolkien, and if it was traceable.

Ruth said the story was told by 'Grandmother' Carr 'in "our" farm kitchen at Blyton Carr in the 1870s' and noted that, according to her Aunt Annie Tongue, the name 'wizard' was interchangeable with 'magician'. The task given to the giant at the end of the story was added to the tale when told by her great-aunt, Miss Hetty Carr, of Blyton Carr Farm, though Ruth had found this as a nature myth attributed to 'Old Scrat', or the Devil.

Blyton Carr is a hamlet situated to the south-west of the village of Blyton, about three miles east of the River Trent, and about two and a half miles north of Gainsborough. The census returns for 1871 show that Elizabeth Carr, Ruth's great-grandmother, by then a widow, farmed 160 acres with the help of two of her children. She died in 1882 at the age of seventy-three, by this time she had moved with her youngest daughter to Sheffield.

THE EAST HALTON HOB-THRUST

In the days of long ago, a farm in Goxhill (or the neighbouring parish of East Halton) was haunted for many years by a hob – an elfin sprite of the Robin Goodfellow type, who used to do all kinds of work about the fields, stackyard and dairy.

It was the farmer's custom on the evening before sheep shearing, to bring his flock into the barn. On one occasion, he neglected to do this and rose early the following morning to carry out the task. However, as he walked out into the yard, he heard the sound of bleating and realised that his sheep were already in the barn.

Rushing inside, he counted the flock and found they had all been brought in from the field, but what was stranger still was the presence among them of a fine full-grown hare. Whilst scratching his head in wonder, and hardly satisfied that he was not dreaming, he heard a shrill voice that made him look upwards suddenly. Perched upon one of the wind beams of the high, pitched roof sat a goblin, who squeaked out a bitter complaint against 'that little grey sheep' that had been more difficult to drive into the barn than all the rest of the flock put together.

In gratitude for his help and goodwill, the farmer promised to give the little creature a linen shirt every New Year's Eve. For this the little creature willingly performed many a piece of nocturnal drudgery.

But over time the farmer either began to think that the help given was not worth the reward given, or he wished in his prosperity to be rid of a servant who was not flesh and blood like himself, and he conceived a plan of dismissal.

On the next New Year's Eve, instead of a linen smock, he left one on the hearth made of the coarsest sacking. This done, the farmer and his family listened in the sleeping loft until the clock struck twelve, when they soon heard the feeble voice of their poor little drudge chanting, half in sorrow and half in anger:

> Harden, harden, harden hemp,
> I will neither grind nor stamp.
> Had you given me linen gear,
> I had served you many a year.
> Thrift may go,
> bad luck may stay,
> I shall travel far away.

And this was the last they ever heard of him. Where he went, they did not know, but one thing was certain, the dairymaids, garthmen, thatchers, and plough lads from that day forward had to do their work unaided, and the farmer's prosperity declined in a way that made him often wish his faithful drudge returned.

A few years later, a lady who was well acquainted with the village confirmed to Mabel Peacock that Manor Farm at East Halton was popularly said to be haunted by a hob-thrust, up until three or four years ago. Her informant believed that the creature's appearance was in some way connected with an old iron cauldron in the cellar, which was full of sand and bones. These bones were supposed to be 'children's thumb bones', and she was told that 'if the bones and sand were stirred, the hob-thrust would show himself at twelve o'clock'. Mabel's informant did not know what the hob had done, but said that the cauldron had been brought up from the cellar to be used, and no evil results had followed. She was also told that there was another hob-thrust at Lindholme, near Wroot.

Leland Lewis Duncan added details from a letter from an East Halton resident in 1893 to say:

> When the S___'s lived on the hill they always burnt a light in one of the bedroom windows to keep Hob-Thrust quiet at night … there is still an iron pot in the cellar which had sand in it, but they took it out and left the pot in the cellar. They have often heard noises in the house like chairs falling and someone coming down stairs and across the floor to the fireplace …

The hob had attracted other common stories. At one time they had tried to build the church in the centre of the village, but each night the hob-thrust destroyed the work done in the daytime, so that they were obliged to build it to the south of the village. It was also said that many years ago, the occupants of the Manor House tried to move and were carting their furniture to their new home when they met a neighbour. When asked where they were going, they replied that they were flitting, and as they said this the hob-thrust popped its head out of an old churn and said, 'Yes, we're flitting.' So the people returned to the farm, and they learnt to get along with the creature that would fetch up the horses each morning, and gather the sheep overnight into the barn for clipping.

Today, tales of the hob are no longer told in connection with Manor Farm; however, the pot mentioned by Mabel Peacock has become the centre of a bigger and darker mystery.

In February 1932, Ethel Rudkin visited the Manor House and was told that it had been very badly haunted, so much so that the inhabitants of the house had felt that something had to be done about it. As a consequence, an iron pot had been put in the cellar, and the malevolent spirit 'laid' in it with a covering of pins and earth. When Rudkin viewed the pot it was in the centre of the floor of a small disused cellar, about 8ft sq., which was reached by means of a stone stairway from one of the lower rooms. Rudkin was also informed, by a previous occupant of the house, that she never moved the pot, as doing so might take away her luck forever.

Over the years this pot has acquired an even more sinister reputation and a newspaper article in the *Lincolnshire Echo* in 1975 alleged that at least three people are said to have died because of the curse attached to the pot.

In 1974, local businessman John Morton had bought the property and had begun extensive renovations, which included breaking into the old cellar. He then found out about the legend when the workmen refused to go anywhere near the corner of the cellar where the battered old pot had lain undisturbed for so long.

The local minister, Revd Bob Kenyon, a firm believer in the curse, heard of the work being carried out and offered to remove the pot, but Mr Morton decided to leave it where it was and surround it with steel plates. The man charged with this unenviable task, local builder Alfred Darwood, said, 'No one really believed the legend but no one would touch it either. We put the steel plates in

without moving the pot. If it had really been in the way,
I suppose we would have had to have moved it. However,
I wouldn't like to have been the one to do it.'

Today, the pot is still sealed in the cellar, but the cellar
itself is also bricked up and inaccessible.

THE FARMER AND THE BOGGART

One day, a boggart came to a man that had bought land
and said to him that he was the proper owner and so the
man must leave. Well, at first the man took no notice
of him whatsoever and pretended that he hadn't seen or
heard him. When he finally got fed up with his wittering
and nagging, he said to the boggart, 'You must take it to
the law if you want to get hold of this land. I won't give it
up till I'm made to.'

The boggart then changed his tune and said, 'I'll tell you
what I'll do. Me and you will go shares. I'll take half the
stuff of the land and you'll take the other half. We won't
have anything to do with them lawyers. I hate them more
than I hate ginger beer that's had the cork left out.'

'Well', the man said, not wanting to make things awk-
ward, 'none but us must settle this first off, and when we've
settled it we must stick to it. Will you take what grows above
ground, or what grows beneath the ground?'

The boggart thought for a minute then said, 'I'll take
what grows above ground, and I'll come and fetch it at harvest time, when you've got everything in.'

The man then thought to himself, 'If I'm to have all that's
beneath the ground, I'll set potatoes. The boggart must take
the potato-tops, and he's welcome to them.'

So when the time came for settling the debt, the boggart arrived to get his share of the crop. The man was ready, and let the boggart have all the piles of couch-grass and potato-tops. But the boggart didn't seem too concerned and said, 'We'll swap. I must have all that grows beneath the ground next time.'

'All right,' said the man. 'Now, you know you must stick to it now you've said it.'

So the man then sowed wheat, and when the boggart came in the fall the man got corn and straw and the boggart got nothing but stubble. At first the boggart was incredibly angry about it, and said that lawyers couldn't do worse than the farmer had done. After a while he calmed down and told the man that next time, they must share the crop out, they must start mowing it together, and each of them must take what he mows.

The man wasn't too worried about this deal, as the boggart looked as strong as a six-year-old horse, and his arms were as long and thin as tackle poles, however, he said to himself that he'd manage to get the better of the boggart. And so he, and the boggart settled the deal and the boggart went away as pleased as a dog with two tails.

But when harvest time came round, the man, who had consulted with a wise man, went to the blacksmith's shop, and got the blacksmith to make him a lot of iron rods, about as thick as clay pipe stems. Then he stuck them amongst the corn that the boggart was to mow, for he'd sewn wheat again that year. And he waited for the boggart to come with his great long scythe, and they set to work.

Before long, the boggart's scythe hit one of the iron rods and he said, 'My word, these stalks are hard to cut.' Then the scythe edge caught another one and he had to stop

to sharpen the blade, and he cursed and swore all the time. Every swing of the scythe made things worse, and the boggart got more and more tired, and at last he said, 'I'm that hot that I must wring my shirt out, let's take a break and have a bit of bacca.'

'Bacca!' says the man. 'What can you be thinking? Why, you haven't mown a quarter of an acre yet. I shan't have a break until eleven, and it's just after eight by the old church clock.'

When the boggart heard this he flung down his scythe and said, 'You may take your land and all that's on it. I won't have anything more to do with it. I'm as sick as a toad of it, and you and all.' And off he went and he never came back.

Folk say that the man took the scythe home with him, and that it is hanging in his barn now, to testify to the truth of his tale.

Some say, however, that the boggart stayed in the area, to scare lonely folks at night, and that if you left your dinner or tools lying around he would often make off with them.

When Mabel Peacock included the story in her *Tales and Rhymes in Lindsey Folk-Speech*, she noted that it was set over the county border in Northamptonshire, and indeed it was included by Sternberg in his *Dialect and Folk-Lore of Northamptonshire* and also in the *Northampton Mercury* in 1886.

However, when Peacock and Eliza Gutch compiled their *Lincolnshire County Folk-Lore*, they noted Robert Heanley as their source and located the tale at Mumby. Lincolnshire-born Revd Heanley related in *The Saga Book of the Viking Club* that this marshland tale was a very significant clue to the 'conquest by the early Britons, or Norsemen, of the dwarf race of prehistoric man'.

Heanley linked the tale to the Irish legend of how the Tuatha Dé Danann were dispossessed by the conquering Milesians. They were given the half that was beneath the earth whilst the new rulers kept Angus, the conquering king, above the ground. The tale also bears a very strong resemblance to the story of 'Jack o' Kent and the Devil', found on the Welsh borders.

4

OF WATER, WIND AND WEATHER

The first three tales in this section were collected by Marie Balfour and formed part of the collection 'The Legends of the Carrs'. She, like most of the members of the Folklore Society, was not just interested in collecting folk tales, but also evidence of the survival of paganism. Such evidence included belief in the supernatural and the power of witches and the making of offerings to pacify the spirits. 'The Dead Moon' is full of references to malevolent entities out on the Carrs at night, as is 'Tiddy Mun'. The latter also includes offerings to the water spirit. The third tale, 'The Green Mist', demonstrates the belief in the power of the spoken word, if heard by the fairy creatures. As previously, I have chosen to keep the tales from 'The Legends of the Carrs' collection as close to the original as possible. These stories will be followed by a short tale about a creature that lives under Pilford Bridge.

This section ends with two tales connected to Lincoln Cathedral, the Devil and the wind. The first is the account of the 'Legend of the Lincoln Imp', including the old ballad based on the same tale, and the second tale describes the origins of the effigy of an imp looking over the shoulder of a woman, which is found above the south porch of the cathedral.

THE DEAD MOON

Long ago, in my gran's time, the Carr lands were all bogs, great pools of black water and creeping trickles of green water, and squishy mud that would suck you in if you stepped on it. My gran used to say, how, long before her time, the moon herself was once dead and buried in the marshes, and I will tell you about it.

The moon up yonder shone and shone then, just as she does now, and when she shone she lit up the bog paths so anybody could walk about, as safe as in the daytime. But when she didn't shine, then out came all the things that dwell in the darkness and went about seeking to do evil and harm to all who were not safe beside their own hearths. Harm, mischance and mischief, bogles and dead things, and crawling horrors; they all came out on those nights when the moon didn't shine.

It so happened that the moon heard of all this and, being kind and good, she said, 'I'll see for myself, I will, if maybe it's not so bad as the folk make out.'

And so, sure enough, come the end of the month down she stepped, wrapped up with a black cloak and a black hood over her yellow shining hair, and went straight to the bog edge and looked about her. Water here and water there, waving tussocks, and trembling mools, and great black snags that twisted and bent; and before her, all dark – dark, but for the glimmer of the stars on the pools, and the light that came from her own white feet stealing out of her black cloak.

On she went to the middle of the bogs, always looking about her, and it was a queer sight that she looked on: the witches grinned as they rode past on their great black cats, the evil eye glowed from the darkest corners, and the will-o'-the-wykes danced all about with their lanterns swinging on their backs. Then the dead folk rose in the water and looked around them, with white twisted faces and hell fire in their empty eye-holes; slimy dripping dead hands slithered about, beckoning and pointing, making her skin crawl.

The moon drew her cloak tighter about her and trembled, but she wouldn't go back without seeing all there was to be seen, and so on she went from tuft to tuft between the greedy gurgling water holes. Just as she came close to a big black pool, her foot slipped and she almost tumbled in – she grabbed with both hands at a snag nearby but as soon as she touched it, it twisted itself round her wrists like a pair of handcuffs and gripped her so she couldn't move. She pulled and twisted and fought but it was no good; she was stuck. She looked about and wondered if help would come by, but she saw nothing but shifting, flurrying evil things.

Presently, she heard something calling in the distance – a voice that called and called and called, and then died away with a sob. But it began again, with a screech of pain and fear, and called and called, till the marshes were full of the pitiful crying voices. Then she heard steps floundering along, squishing in the muck and slipping on the tufts, and through the darkness she saw hands catching at the snags and the tussocks, and a white face with great fearful eyes.

It was a man who had strayed into the bogs, and all around him the grinning bogles, the dead, and the creeping horrors crawled and crowded; the voices mocked him, and the dead hands plucked at him, and ahead the will-o'-the-wykes dangled their lanterns and shook with evil glee as they led him further and further from the right track. Confused with fear and loathing for the things about him, he struggled on towards the flickering lights that looked like help and safety.

'You over there,' he shrieked. 'You! I'm caught in the boglands! Do you hear? God and Mary save us from the Horrors – help – you over there!' And then he'd stop and sob and moan and call on all the saints and wise women and God himself to fetch him out.

When the poor moon saw that he was coming nearer and nearer to the deep holes and further and further from the path, she was so mad and so sorry, that she struggled and fought and pulled harder than ever. And though she couldn't get loose, with all her twisting and tugging, the black hood fell back off her shining yellow hair and the beautiful light that came from it drove away the darkness.

At once the evil things fled back into the dark corners, for they cannot abide the light. The man could now see where he was and where the path was, and where he'd have to go to get away from the boglands and the things that dwelt there. He scarce looked at the brave light that came from the beautiful shining yellow hair streaming out over the black cloak, and falling to the water at his feet. And the moon herself was so took up with saving him and with rejoicing that he was back on the right path, that she clean forgot that she needed help herself, and that she was held fast by the snag.

So off he went, gasping and stumbling, and sobbing with joy, fleeing for his life out of the terrible bogs. Then it came over the moon that she'd like to go with him: and a great fear came to her; and she pulled and fought as if she was mad, till she fell on her knees at the foot of the snag.

And as she lay there, gasping for breath, the black hood fell forward over her head; and though she tried to throw it back, it was caught in her hair, and wouldn't go. So out went the light, and back came the darkness with all its evil things, with a screech and a howl. They came crowding round her, mocking and snatching and beating; shrieking with rage and spite, and swearing with foul tongues, spitting and snarling, for they knew her for their old enemy, the brave bright moon. The poor moon crouched trembling and sick, and wondered when they would make an end of it and of her.

'Damn you!' yelled the witch-bodies, 'you've spoiled our spells!'

'And you keeps us in our straight coffins at nights!' moaned the dead folk.

'And you send us to brood in the corners!' howled the bogles.

And all the things joined in with a great 'Ho, ho!' till the very tussocks shook and the water gurgled.

'We'll poison her – poison her!' shrieked the witches.

And 'Ho, ho!' howled the things again.

'We'll smother her – smother her!' whispered the crawling horrors, and twined themselves around her knees.

And 'Ho, ho!' mocked the rest of them.

'We'll strangle her – strangle her!' screeched the dead hands, and plucked at her throat with cold fingers.

And 'Ho, ho!' they yelled again.

But the dead folk writhed and grinned about and they chuckled to themselves. 'We'll bury thee, bury thee, down with us in the black mools!'

And again they shouted with spite and ill-will. The poor moon crouched down and wished she was dead and done with.

The things fought and squabbled over what they should do with her, till the sky changed to a pale grey and it drew near to dawn. When they saw that, they were afraid lest they shouldn't have time to work their will; and they caught hold of her, with their horrid bony fingers, and laid her deep in the water at the foot of the snag. The dead folk held her down while the bogles sought a great big stone and rolled it on top of her, to keep her from rising. They told two of the will-o'-the-wykes to take turns in watching on the black snag, to see that she lay safe and still and couldn't get out to spoil their sport with her light, or to help the poor Carr folk to keep out of the quicks and holes of nights. And then, as the grey light came brighter in the sky, the shapeless things fled away to seek the dark corners, and the dead folk crept back into the water, or crammed themselves into their coffins, and the witches went home to their ill-doings.

And the green slimy water shone in the dawning as if no ill thing would come near it.

And there lay the poor moon, buried in the bog until someone could set her loose; and who would know where to look for her?

Well, the days passed and it was time for the new moon's coming; the folk put pennies in their pockets and straws in their caps so as to be ready for it, and looked about quietly, for the moon was a good friend to the marsh folk.

But days and days passed, and the new moon never came. The nights were dark, and the evil things were worse than ever. There were no roads safe to travel, and the boggarts crept and wailed around the houses and looked in at the windows and snapped at the latches, till the poor people had to keep their lights on at night, else the horrors would come over their very doorsills.

Aye so, the bogles seemed to have lost all their fear; they howled and laughed and screeched around, fit to wake the dead themselves. The Carr folk would sit trembling and shaking by the fire, and could not sleep nor rest, nor put a foot across the sill, on the dark and dreary nights.

And still the days went on and the new moon never came.

Naturally, the Carr folk were afraid and bewildered, and a lot of them went to the wise woman, who dwelt in the old mill, and asked if she could find out where the moon had gone.

'Well,' said she, after looking in the brewpot and in the mirror and in the book, 'it be really odd, but I can't rightly tell you what's happened with her. It is dark, dark, and I cannot see anything in the spells. Go slow, children, I'll think about it, and maybe I can help you yet. If you hear of anything, come by and tell me; and anyway, put a pinch of salt, a straw, and a button on the doorsill at nights, and the horrors won't be able to come over it, light or no light.'

As the days went by, never a moon came, naturally they talked! Their tongues wagged like I don't know what, at home, and at the inn, and in the garth. And one day, as they sat on the great settle in the inn, a man from the far end of the boglands was smoking and listening, when all at once he sat up and slapped his knee – my word! – 'I'd clean forgot, but I reckon I know where the moon is!' And he told them how he was lost in the bogs, and how, when he nearly died of fright, the light shone out, and all the evil things fled away, and he found the path and got home safe.

'And I was so confused with fear,' said he, 'I didn't rightly look where the light came from, but I remember well, it was soft and white like the moon herself. And it came from something dark standing near a black snag in the water. And I didn't rightly look, but I seem to remember a shining face and yellow hair in the middle of the dazzle, and it had a sort of kind look, like the old moon herself above the Carrs at night.'

So off they went to the wise woman and told her about it, and she looked long into the pot and at the book again, and then she nodded her head.

'It's dark still, children, dark!' says she. 'And I can't rightly see anything, but do as I tell you. Go, all of you, just before the night gathers, put a stone in your gobs, and take a hazel twig in your hands and say not a word till you are safe home again. Then walk into the middle of the marsh until you find a coffin, a cross and a candle. Then you'll not be far from your moon.'

They looked at each other, and scratched their heads.

'But where will we find her, mother?' says one.

'And how will we go?' says the other.

'And will none of the bogles get us?' says another, and so on.

'Fools!' said she, annoyed like. 'Parcel of fools! I can tell you no more; do as I tell you and fear nothing; and if you don't want to, then stay at home and do without your moon.'

The next night at twilight, every man went out with a stone in his mouth and a hazel twig in his hand, feeling very afraid. They stumbled and tottered along the paths into the middle of the bogs. They saw nothing, though they heard sighing and flustering in their ears and felt cold wet fingers touching them. But on they went, looking around for the coffin, the candle, and the cross until they came near to the pool beside the great snag, where the moon lay buried.

And at once they saw the great stone, half in, half out of the water, looking for the entire world like a big strange coffin; and at the head was the black snag, stretching out its two arms in a dark gruesome cross; and on it a tiddy light flickered, like a dying candle. They knelt down in the muck, crossed themselves and said, 'Our Lord' – first forward, because of the cross, then backward, to keep off the bogles – but without speaking out, for they knew that the evil things would catch them, if they didn't do as the wise woman said.

Then they went nearer, took hold of the big stone and shoved it up, and for one tiddy minute they saw a strange and beautiful face looking up at them gratefully out of the black water. But the light came so quick and so white and shining, that they stepped back amazed by it, and with the great angry wail that came from the fleeing horrors. When they could see again, there was the full moon in the sky, bright and beautiful and kind as ever, shining and smiling down at them and making the bogs and the paths as clear as day, stealing into the very corners to drive the darkness and the bogles clean away.

The Carr folk went home with light hearts, and ever since that night the moon shines brighter and clearer over the bogs than anywhere, for the moon remembered well that the horrors come with the dark, and that the Carr folk sought her and found her when she was buried in the bog. And mark my words, it be true, for my gran herself had seen the snag with its two arms like a great cross and the green slimy water at its foot, where the poor moon was buried, and the stone nearby that kept her down.

'The Dead Moon' was told by 'a young girl of nine ... who stated that she had heard it from her "gran".' The same girl – known as 'Fanny' – also told the tale of 'Sam'l's Ghost', which forms the concluding part of the story of 'Fred the Fool'.

Joseph Jacobs included an abridged version of this story in his *More English Fairy Tales*, under the revised name of 'The Buried Moon'. Jacobs also provided the information from Marie that the narrator's surname was Bratton. My research suggests that the girl was called Agnes Brattan and she lived at Stoneham in Redbourne.

Katharine Briggs believed that this story is not commonly found in Europe. However, in *The Clouds* by Aristophanes there is mention of the 'hiring of a Thessalian witch to bring down the moon and shut her up in a box'. The story also bears similarities to the 'Kalevala' rune 49, in which the moon is stolen and trapped (along with the sun).

The story 'Well in the Well', from Yorkshire, also shares features with this tale. Our Lady's Well near Threshfield in north-west Yorkshire was regarded as a place of protection from supernatural creatures such as hobs, witches, goblins and boggarts. One day, a man on his way home saw 'a ghost and a number of wicked imps and goblins engaged in a wild and weird dance'. He stood still and watched but then accidentally sneezed. The spirits began to chase after him with 'hue and cry'. He leapt into the well and remained there whilst the creatures surrounded the well until cockcrow.

TIDDY MUN

Since before the dykes were made and the riverbed changed, when the Carrs were nothing but boglands and full of waterholes, they were teeming at night with boggarts and wil-o'-the-wikes, voices of the dead folk and hands without arms, todlowries dancing on the tussocks, and witches riding on the great black snags. Folk were scared of these creatures and wouldn't go near them without a charm of some sort.

The people shook with fright when they found themselves in the Carrs at twilight. They were mostly shaking in those times anyway; the women over the fire, the men out in the yard, even the babies, for the marsh fever was bad. They were poor weak creatures then, fit for nothing but to drink gin and eat opium.

They knew that the fever came from the bogs, but when they heard that the marshes must be drained they were very discontented, for they were used to them and they thought, as the saying goes, 'bad's bad, but meddling's worse'.

The people were told that the mists would lift and the bogs would turn into earth, and there'd be no marsh fever; but they disliked the changes, and were very angry with the Dutchmen who came across the seas for the drainage.

The folk would not give the Dutchmen refreshments or bedding or fair words, and they said to each other that it would be ill days for the Carrs, and the poor Carr folk, if the bog holes were messed with and Tiddy Mun annoyed.

For they knew that Tiddy Mun dwelt in the waterholes down deep in the green still water, and he came creeping out only in the twilight, when the mists rose, limpelty-lobelty, like a dear wee old grandfather, cloaked in grey, with long white hair and a long white beard, all matted and tangled together. He arrived with a sound of running water and a gust of wind, and laughter like the pyewipe screech. They called him Tiddy Mun, for he was no bigger than a three-year-old baby, and he didn't have a real name – he never had had.

They were not as scared of Tiddy Mun as they were of boggarts and the dead hands, though. But nevertheless, they were sort of shivery like when they sat round the fire, to hear the screeching laugh out by the door, passing in a shriek of wind and water; still they only moved in a bit nearer together, and listened with a look over their shoulder, 'Listen to Tiddy Mun!'

Mind you, the old Mun hurt no one, no, he were really good to us at times. When the year was getting wet and the water rose in the marshes, and it crept up to the doorsill and covered the paths, come the first new moon, the father and mother, and the children, would go out in the twilight and, looking over the bog, would call out together: 'Tiddy Mun, without a name, the waters through!'

And they would all hold hands and tremble, and shake and shiver, as they heard the old Mun's call, like the pyewipe screech across the swamp!

And in the morning, sure enough, the water would be down and the paths dry. Tiddy Mun had done the job for them.

He lived in the waterholes, and now the Dutchmen were emptying them out, and the people remember the old rhyme, that says:

> Tiddy Mun, without a name
> White head, walking lame;
> While the water teems the fen
> Tiddy Mun'll harm none.

And this was the problem! For the waterholes were now dry, and the water had been drawn off into big dykes so that the quivering bog was turning into firm soil, and where would Tiddy Mun hide then? Everybody said that ill times were coming for the Carrs.

But there was no stopping the Dutchmen; they worked hard and drew the water off, and the dykes got ever longer and longer, and deeper and deeper; the water ran away, and ran away down to the river, and the black soft boglands would soon be turned to green fields. Though the work got done, it was not without trouble. At the inn of nights, on the great settle, and in the yards and in the kitchens at home, the people heard strange and queer tales. The old folk wagged their heads and the young ones wagged their tongues, and the ancients thought and the others said, 'For sure, it is ill comes of crossing Tiddy Mun!'

It was not long before one of the Dutchmen was spirited away! Not a sight of him anywhere! They sought for him and sought for him, but not a shadow of him was ever seen again, and the Carr folk knew that they would never find him; not even if they sought till the end of time.

Tiddy Mun had taken him away and drowned him in the mud holes where they hadn't drawn off all the water! And the Carr folk nodded and said: 'Ay, that's what comes of crossing Tiddy Mun!'

But they brought more Dutchmen for the work, and though Tiddy Mun took them and took them, the work went on and there was no stopping it, and soon the poor Carr folk knew that the old Mun was angry with everybody, not just the Dutchmen, for soon the land dried out, and the cows pined, the pigs starved, the ponies went lame, the babies got sick, the lambs faded away, the frumenty burnt, the new milk curdled, the thatch fell in, and the walls burst out, and all went arsy-varsy!

At first the Carr folk couldn't imagine that Tiddy Mun would worry the people in such a way, and they blamed the witches and the fairies. So the lads stoned the cross-eyed witch at Gorby, and Sally at Wadham with the evil eye, who charmed the dead men out of their graves; they ducked her in the horse pond until she was almost dead; and they all said the 'Our Father' backwards and spat to the east to keep the tod-lowries' pranks off; but it did not help; for Tiddy Mun himself was angry and he was visiting it on the poor Carr folks. And what could they do?

The babies sickened in their mothers arms, and their poor white faces never brightened up; the fathers sat and smoked, while the mothers wept over the innocent babies. It was like a frost that comes and kills the bonniest flowers. But their hearts were sore, and their stomachs empty with all this sickness and bad harvest, and they knew something must be done, or the Carr folk would soon be dead and gone.

Anyway, some of them remembered how, when the waters rose in the marshes before the drainage, the folk would go out at new moon in the twilight and call to Tiddy Mun. And they thought, maybe if they called him again and showed him that the Carr folk wished him well, and that they would give him the water back if they only could, that maybe he would forgive them and undo the bad spell.

So they fixed it that they should all meet together at the next new moon down by the cross dyke, near the old post by John Ratton's yard.

Well, it was a regular gathering of all the Carr folk – the men and women and bairns. They came in threes and fours, jumping at every sigh of wind, and screeching at every snag, but they didn't need to for the poor old boggarts and jack o' lanterns were clean drained away.

They came, every one with a jug of fresh water in their hand, and as it grew dark they all stood together, listening and looking over their shoulders, and harkening uneasy-like to the sound of the wind and the lip-lap of the running water.

As dusk began to fall at last, they stood at the dyke-edge, and looked over to the new river, and they called out together, strange and loud:

Tiddy Mun, without a name,
Here's water for thee,
take the spell undone!

And they poured the water out of the jugs in the dyke.

The people were getting scared by now, standing holding on together in the stillness. They listened with all their might to hear if Tiddy Mun answered them; but there was nothing but unnatural stillness. And then, just when they began to fear that it was all for nothing, they heard the most awful wailing and whimpering all around them; like little crying babies weeping as if to break their hearts, and none to comfort them. They sobbed and sobbed quietly, and then began again louder than ever, wailing and moaning until they made the folk's hearts ache to hear them.

And as they thought of their dead babies, the mothers cried out, calling on Tiddy Mun to take the spell away and let the children live and grow strong; and the poor innocents, floating above in the twilight, moaned and whimpered softly, as if they knew their mothers' voices and were trying to reach their bosom. And there were women who said that little hands had touched them, and cold lips kissed them, and soft wings fluttered round them that night, as they stood waiting and listening to the woeful greeting.

Then all at once, there was stillness again, and they could hear the water lapping at their feet and the dog yapping in the yard. But then there came, soft and gentle from the river, the old pyewipe screech. Once and again it came and they recognised the old Mun's call; they knew that he'd taken the spell away, for he sounded so kind and caring.

Oh how they laughed and cried together, running and jumping about like a pack of children coming out of school.

They set off for home with light hearts and never a thought of the boggarts. Only the mothers thought of their dead babies and their arms felt empty, their hearts lonesome and weary with thinking of their poor wee bodies, drifting about in the sighing of the night wind.

From that day, things thrived in the Carrs: the sick babies got well, the cattle flourished, the bacon-pigs fattened, the men folk earned good wages, and there was plenty of food, for Tiddy Mun had taken the bad spell away. And in twilight at every new moon, out the Carr folk went to the nearest dyke edge, father, mother and children, and they poured the water in the dyke crying:

> Tiddy Mun wi-out a name
> Here's water for thee!

And the pyewipe screech would come back, soft and tender and pleased. But if one of them didn't go out, except if they were sick, Tiddy Mun missed them, and was angry with them and laid the spell on them harder than ever; until they went with the others, come next new moon, to ask for the spell to be undone. And when the children misbehaved, they said Tiddy Mun would take them away; and the children became as good as gold, for they knew he would do it.

But those days have gone now, and folk now know little about him. I guess Tiddy Mun's been frightened away with all the new ways, and I never hear anyone say now, as we used to say when I was young, if anybody had a lot of trouble and mischance, and wry luck, 'Ah, thou haven't been out in the new moon lately, and for certain-sure, it's ill to cross Tiddy Mun without a name!'

This Carrs story was told to her by a lady who was in her late seventies, and as such includes some beautifully antiquated language. Marie Balfour included the fact that the narrator had died before the publication of the tale in *Folklore* in 1891, and this enabled me to carry out research on who it may have been.

From my research, I have concluded that the narrator was Mary Whelpton, who was born in Redbourne village in 1808, to a family who had lived in the Carrs for generations. She and her husband John (who died two years before her in 1887) had four children, and their eldest daughter remained in the village with her own children and grandchildren. Mary also cared for at least two of her grandchildren by another daughter who died in 1879.

I would also like to point out that the descriptions within the narrative of the drainage, the ecological consequences and the opium use by the people are factually supported. A very informative paper on the effect of the drainage on the Carrs was inlcuded in the journal *Folklore* in 1987 by Darwin Horn.

It can also be said that the folklorist Ethel Rudkin believed in 'Tiddymun', and described him as a friendly creature to those who lived locally, but to foreigners he was an evil old man and not pleasant. Similarly the fear that creatures living in the water would pull you under was widespread in the marsh and fen district.

Regarding the folklore content of the tale, Mabel Peacock noted that, 'It is still considered natural that the descendants of people who enclosed common land at the end of the eighteenth and beginning of the nineteen centuries, should suffer from ill-luck.' Peacock gave the example of a family whose ancestors had enclosed a stretch of poor quality moorland and turned it into rich farmland, much to the annoyance of local cottagers who had common rights on it. The descendants of the cottagers believed that the family had not 'thriven'.

THE GREEN MIST

In the old times, folk must have been different than now. Instead of doing their work in the days and smoking their pipes on Sundays in peace and comfort, they were always bothering their heads about something or other – or the church were doing it for them.

The priests were always at them about their souls; and what with hell and the boggarts, their minds were never easy. There were things that didn't belong to the church and folk had ideas of their own and ways of their own that they had kept up for hundreds of years, since the time when there wasn't a church; a time when they gave things to the bogles and such, to keep them friendly.

My grandfather said that the bogles had once been thought of a lot more, and at twilight every night the folk would carry lights in their hands round their houses, and they would smear blood on the doorsill to scare away the horrors; that they would put bread and salt on the flat stones set up by the lane side to get a good harvest, and they would spill water in the four corners of the fields when they wanted rain. They thought a lot about the sun, for they reckoned that it made the earth, and brought the good and ill chances and I don't know what else.

I can't tell you what they believed, for it was before even my grandfather's time, and that's more than a hundred and fifty years ago, you see. But I reckon they made nearly everything that they saw and heard into sort of great bogles; and they were always giving them things, or saying sort of prayers like, to keep them from doing the folk any evil.

Well, that was a long time ago, and it was not so bad in my grandfather's day but nevertheless, it wasn't forgot, and some of the folk believed it all still, and said their prayers or spells like in secret. So, there were two churches; the one with priests and candles, and the other just a lot of old ways, kept up secretly amongst the folk themselves. They thought a lot more of the old spells, than on the service in the church itself. But as time went on the two got sort of mixed up, and some of the folks couldn't have told you if it was for one or the other that they did things.

At Yule, in the churches there were grand services, with candles and flags and what not, and in the cottages there were candles and cakes and grand doings; but the priests never knew that many of the folk were only waking the dying year, and that the wine poured upon the doorsill at first cockcrow was to bring good luck in the new year. I reckon some of the folk themselves would do the old heathen ways and sing hymns meantime, with never a thought of the strangeness of it.

Still, there were many that kept to the old ways altogether, though they did it hidden like; and I am going to tell you of one family that my grandfather knew well, and how they woke the earth one year.

As I said before, I can't, even if I could, tell you all the things that they use to do, but there was one time of the year when they particularly went in for their spells and prayers, and that was the early spring. They thought that the earth was sleeping all the winter, and that the bogles – call them what you will – had nothing to do but mischief, for they had nothing to see to in the fields. They were afraid on the long dark winter days and nights, in the middle of all sorts of unseen fearsome things ready and waiting for a chance to play their evil tricks. But as the winter went by they thought that it was time to wake the earth from its slumber and set the bogles to work, caring for the growing of crops and bringing the harvest. After that, the earth was tired and would sink to sleep again, and they would sing husherby songs in the fields in the autumn evenings.

When spring arrived they went – the folk that believed in the old ways – to every field in turn and lifted a spade of earth, and they said strange and queer words that they could scarcely understand themselves – the same words that had been said for hundreds of years. And every morning, at first dawn, they stood on the doorsill with salt and bread in their hands, watching and waiting for the green mist that rose from the fields and told them that the earth was awake again; that life was coming to the trees and the plants, and the seeds were bursting with the beginning of the spring.

Well, there was one family that had done all that, year after year, for as long as they knew of, just as their grandfathers had done before them. One winter evening, nigh on a hundred and thirty years ago now, they were making ready for waking the spring. They had a lot of trouble through the winter, sickness and what not had been bad in that place, and the daughter, a ramping young maid, had grown white and weak like a bag of bones, instead of being the prettiest lass in the village as she had been before. Day after day she grew whiter and weaker, till she couldn't stand upon her feet more than a newborn, and she could only lay at the window watching and watching the winter creep away.

'Oh mother,' she had kept saying over and over again, 'if I could only wake the spring with you again, maybe the green mist would make me strong and well, like the trees and the flowers and the corn in the fields.'

And the mother would comfort her and promise that she would come with them again to the waking, and grow strong and straight as ever. But day after day she got whiter and weaker, till she looked, my grandfather said, like a snow-flake fading in the sun; and day after day the winter crept by, and the waking of the spring were almost there. The poor maid watched and waited for the time for going to the fields, but she had got so weak and sick that she knew she couldn't get there with the rest. But she wouldn't give up for all that; and her mother swore that she would lift the lass to the doorsill, at the coming of the green mist, so that she might toss out the bread and salt of the earth herself with her own poor thin hands.

And still the days went by, and the folk were going out early in the morning to lift the spade in the fields; and the coming of the green mist was looked for every dawn. And one evening the lass, who had been laying with her eye fixed on the little garden, said to her mother, 'If the green mist don't come in the morning's dawning, I'll not wait for it any longer. The mools are calling me, and the seeds are bursting that will bloom over my bed; I know it well mother – and yet, if I could only see the spring wake once again, mother, I swear I'd ask no more than to live as long as one of them cowslips that come every year by the gate, and to die with the first of them when the summer's in.'

The mother shushed the maid in fear, for the bogles and things that they believed in were always nearby and could hear all that was said. The poor folk were never safe, never alone, not with the things that they couldn't see and couldn't hear always round them.

But the dawn of the next day brought the green mist. It came from the mools and wrapped itself round everything, green as grass in summer sunshine, and sweet-smelling as the herbs of the spring. The lass was carried to the doorsill, where she crumbled the bread and salt on to the earth with her own hand and said the strange old words to welcome the new spring. She looked to the gate where the cowslips grew, and then was taken back to her bed by the window, where she slept like a baby and dreamt of summer and flowers and happiness. For whether it was the green mist had done it, I can't tell you more than my grandfather said, but from that day she grew stronger and prettier than ever, and by the time the cowslips were budding she was running about, and laughing like a sunbeam in the old cottage.

But she was still always so white and wan, and she looked like a will-o-the-wyke flitting about. On the cold days she would sit shaking over the fire, and she would look nigh dead, but when the sun came out, she would dance and sing in the light, and stretch out her arms to it as if she only lived in the warmness of it.

And by and by the cowslips burst their buds, and came in flower, and the maid had grown so strange and beautiful that they were afraid of her – and every morning she would kneel by the cowslips and water and tend them and dance to them in the sunshine, while the mother would stand begging her to leave them, and cried that she'd have them pulled up by the roots and thrown away.

But the lass had only to look strange at her and say, soft and low like, 'If you aren't tired of me mother, never pick one of them flowers; they'll fade on their own soon enough – yes, soon enough – you know!'

And the mother would go back to the cottage and weep over the work, but she never said anything of her trouble to the neighbours – not till afterwards.

But one day a lad of the village stopped at the gate to chat with her and by and by, while they were gossiping he picked a cowslip and played with it. The lass didn't see what he had done, but as he said goodbye she saw the flower that had fallen to the earth at his feet. 'Did thee pull that cowslip?' she said, looking strange and white, with one hand over her heart.

'Ay' said he, lifting it up and giving it to her, smiling like, and thinking what a pretty maid she was.

She looked at the flower and at the lad, and all round about her – at the green trees, the sprouting grass, the yellow blossoms, and up at the golden shining sun itself – and all at once, shrinking as if the light she had loved so much were burning her, she ran into the house without a spoken word, only a sort of cry, like a dumb beast in pain, the cowslip clutched close against her breast.

And then – believe it or not – she never spoke again, but lay on the bed, staring at the flower in her hand and fading, as it faded all through the day. At dawn there was only a wrinkled, white, shrunken dead thing laying on the bed and within her hand a shrivelled cowslip. The mother covered it over with the clothes and thought of the beautiful joyful maid dancing like a bird in the sunshine by the golden nodding blossoms.

The bogles had heard her and had given her wish; she had bloomed with the cowslips and had faded with the first of them. My grandfather said, 'It was all as true as death!'

Marie Balfour revealed little about the man who told her this tale. My research has shown that, whilst there may have been some exaggeration, a number of the folklore elements within the tale – the offerings made to the land and the significance of cowslips – have been proven to have existed in Lincolnshire. Folklorist Maureen Sutton found that at the time of the spring equinox 'it was once the custom in the county to celebrate the first day of spring by awakening the sleeping spirits in the earth'. At Swineshead it was 'the custom for farmers to throw four clods of earth across the field to wake the sleeping spirits in the earth …'

Lady Gomme speculated that the game played by young children, Oats and Beans and Barley Grow, which was found in many places including Lincolnshire, 'preserved the traditions of a formula sung at the sowing of grain, in order to propitiate the earth goddess to promote and quicken the growth of the crops'. It is also noticeable that more than one clergyman was to comment, in the mid- to late nineteenth century, on the mix of Paganism and Christianity within the county.

THE POTTED WITCH OF PILFORD BRIDGE

Like the malevolent spirit at Manor Farm, East Halton, mentioned in an earlier story, it is also said that a hostile entity was put into a pot and placed in the water under Pilford Bridge. The bridge crosses the River Ancholme in a small valley between Toft-next-Newton and Normanby-by-Spital.

Ethel Rudkin was informed that the entity was a witch, not a live one, but the spirit of one that haunted the bridge and pushed people into the river. The story was told that three parsons were called to settle the spirit. As each of the parsons stood on the riverbank they asked the spirit what 'she' wanted. 'Life I want, and life I'll have,' she replied.

The men then threw a live cockerel into the river, and the spirit started to tear it limb from limb, and had soon devoured it. The parsons then took a big pot and put it over the spirit, imprisoning her inside. It was believed that if the pot was raised the creature would 'come out again and be as bad as ever'.

THE LEGEND OF THE LINCOLN IMP

On the hill in Lincoln stands one of the finest cathedrals in the world, but because much of the county is flat, the wind constantly blows round this wonderful building. Inside the building the architecture is magnificent, however, there are a number of grotesque carvings hidden amongst the more glorious pieces. A particularly fine example is a carved imp set alongside twenty-eight carved angels, high up above the Angel Choir.

If you look above the penultimate east column on the north side of the Angel Choir you can see the small hairy bodied imp sitting impertinently with one leg carelessly crossed over the other, and with both hands holding the raised leg. An even closer look will show that he has just three thick fingers on each hand, he is baring his sharp teeth, and his bull ears beneath his bull horns are cocked.

It is fitting that the imp should be located on the north side of the choir as this is the side associated with hell and the Devil.

A legend survives within the county of how this imp came to be here, and of why the wind keeps blowing outside, however, there is a rhyme that gives a beautifully graphic account and I have chosen to include that, rather than rewriting the tale. The rhyme seems to have first appeared in print in 1903 in a book by Cora B Forbes. A year after this, H.J. Kesson produced a delightful little illustrated book with an extended version of the rhyme with a moral. This is the former:

The Devil was in a good humour one day,
And let out his sprightly young demons to play.
One dived in the sea and was not at all wet;
One jumped in a furnace, no scorch did he get;
One rode on a rainbow; one delved in the dirt;
One handled forked lightning, nor got any hurt;
One rode on the wind as he would on a steed,
and thus to 'Old Lindum' was carried with speed.

'And now,' says the Imp, 'take me into the church,
His Lordship of Lindum we'll knock off his perch.
We'll blow up the Chapter, and blow up the Dean,
The Canons I'll cannon right over the screen.
We'll blow up the singers, bass, tenor and boy,
And the blower himself shall a blowing enjoy.
The organist, too, shall right speedily find
That I'll go one better in raising the wind.
We'll blow out the windows, and blow out the lights,
Tear vestments to tatters, put ritual to rights!

Now the wind has his faults, but you'll find on the whole,
If somewhat uncouth, he's an orthodox soul;
He wouldn't blow hard on a Monarch, I ween,
Nor ruffle the robes of a Bishop or Dean;
And if for Dissenters he cares not the least,
You won't catch him blowing up Deacon or Priest.
The man in the street he may rudely unrig,
But he snatches not Judge's or Barrister's wig.
When he enters a church, as the musical know,
'Tis only to make the sweet organ-pipes blow.
So in sorrowful anger he said to the elf,
'No! Here I shall stop, you may go by yourself.'

The impudent Imp in derision replied,
'Such half-hearted folks are much better outside.
To force you to enter I cannot, but see,
Till I've finished my fun, you must wait here for me.'

Then he entered the porch in an imp-ious way,
Declaring the nave should be spelt with a K;
He roamed through each transept, he strolled in each aisle,
Then he thought in the choir he would romp for a while.
As he passed 'neath the rood no obeisance he made,
No rev'rence at all to the altar he paid;
He thumbed both the Priest's and the Choristers' books,
And cast on the saints his most insolent looks.
The chalice and patens were safe in a box.
He was stopped in the act of unpicking the locks.
For, seeing some angels he cried, 'Pretty things,
A sackful of feathers I'll pluck from your wings,
To make me a couch when I'm tired of this joke.'
Ah! Soon he was sorry that rudely he spoke;
For the tiniest angel, in dignified tone
Cried 'Imp-ious Imp, be ye turned into stone!'
As he was, as you'll see when to Lincoln you stray:
And the wind has been waiting outside till this day
You can't see the wind, but no matter for that:
Believe! Or he'll rob you of cloak or of hat.

The Devil Looking Over Lincoln

Also on the outside, above the south porch of the bishop's door of Lincoln Cathedral, can be found an effigy of another imp looking over the shoulder of a woman.

The story connected with this has two imps travelling to the majestic building and flying round enjoying themselves. Eventually they became separated, one outside and one inside the building. The imp who was outside became tired, and seeing a witch's back that was humped and fairly broad, he dropped down and settled quietly so that he didn't startle the hag. However, on landing he was turned to stone and has remained in the present position ever since. The effigy is now known as 'The Devil Looking over Lincoln'.

Simpson noted that the story of the imp is also found at Coutances in Normandy. Lincolnshire County Council, in recognition of the importance of the Lincoln Imp and the legends attached to it, have a stylised version of the imp as their logo. Similarly, Lincoln City Football Club has a giant imp as the club mascot.

5

OF WITCHES, WIZARDS, WRAITHS AND WEREWOLVES

Mabel Peacock found that there was much belief in, and fear of, witches, wizards, and wise men and women in Lincolnshire. She declared that she had 'been acquainted with at least four people suspected of "knowing more than they should"'. Her father, Edward Peacock, noted that these wise men and women were 'those who practise beneficial magic'. James Penny similarly recorded lots of evidence for wise men, wise women and witches in the Horncastle area, a number of them with good reputations for helping people. Ethel Rudkin also found testimonies for thirteen witch cases, as well as for two wise men/wizards.

Within this section I will relate a number of tales connected to witchcraft, along with an allegedly true account of a werewolf. The first tale is the most well known, and is kept 'alive' by the maintenance of the horseshoes which mark the site where the horse Byard leapt into the air with a witch on his back. After a brief selection of more tales of witches and

wise men, the section will end with a tale of the popular custom of watching the church pirch on St Mark's Eve.

The Legend of Byard's Leap

In the midst of what was once a lonely tract of high land called Ancaster Heath, ran the old Roman road from Ancaster to Lincoln (now known as the High Dyke or Viking Way). On the eastern side of this road was a farmhouse known as Byard's Leap. About fifty yards north of this old building, near a pond by the roadside, can be found two sets of four very large iron horseshoes, embedded in the ground.

About four hundred years ago, in a local cave there lived a vindictive old witch named Meg. All the local people were wary of her and did her bidding, for if they did not she would get her revenge. She could addle the milk, turn the ale sour, make the cows drop their calves and even give a baby a squint with just a look. Things came to a head when a baby was stillborn to a woman who had turned the witch away from her house. The local people hatched a plan to trap the witch,

and the local shepherd was chosen to help as it was rumoured that he was on intimate terms with the old woman. In fact, it was said that he was too afraid to break off relations with the witch, for fear of the consequences.

At last they were ready 'to get shot of her' and a plan was hatched: in the evening the shepherd would lead the farm horses to water at the pond by the roadside, opposite the hag's den. He would then throw a stone into the water as the horses were drinking, and watch to see which horse raised its head first. The young man was then to climb onto the back of this horse and call for the old woman to climb up behind him. When she did so, he would stab her with a two-edged knife as if in self-defence. Old Meg, in the struggle, would fall into the pond and be drowned, and so die in the way common to witches.

As darkness was just beginning to fall the young shepherd did as he had been told. He led the horses to the water, threw a stone into the pond and then climbed onto the back of the horse that had raised its head. This horse was in fact blind Byard, which was fortunate because a normal horse would shrink from contact with the witch.

Seated on the horse, the shepherd then called for Old Meg to join him. When she heard his call, instead of coming out, she replied, 'Wait till I've buckled my shoes and suckled the cubs, and I'll be with you.'

The shepherd stayed where he was and waited while the witch fed her two ill-formed children. In time she came out and climbed onto the horse. The lad plunged the knife into the old hag's breast and she, in agony, dug her sharp fingernails into the horse's back.

Blind Byard at once made a wild, sudden leap, which unseated the witch and took him 60ft from the spot. The horse then made a second leap, as large as the first to the place that is now marked by four horseshoes, and the witch fell into the pond, and drowned, as planned.

Ethel Rudkin was informed that the man chosen to attack the witch was an old soldier from Ancaster who had returned from the wars with his horse, Old Blind Bayard. Three times he had tried the experiment of throwing the stone into the water, and each time it was his horse that had turned its head. He rode to the witch's house and waited whilst she 'suckled her cubs' and then he severed one of her breasts. This act drove her into a fury and she leapt onto the horse and dug her fingers and toes into the animal, such that it made three giant leaps. The witch clung on until the soldier turned and ran her through with his sword, piercing Old Bayard too. The witch and her 'cubs' were said to be buried under a nearby stone, which looks like a mounting block.

Ethel noted that the story was widely told in Lincolnshire, and that there was a field at Ashby Lodge Farm, known as 'Meg's Hole', where it was said that the witch spent time and also died.

Sidney Addy found a version of the tale that was set near Market Rasen and which included a wise man who gave advice to farmers that wished to be rid of a local witch. During the attempt, the witch's arm was grazed by the dagger and the horse leapt seven yards on each of three leaps. After this, the witch lost her powers. Another account has the witch named as 'Old Meg' and the attacker 'Big Jim'. A further account has the witch living in the farmhouse; another has it that she, when attacked, turned into a lion. The most interesting thing about the legend, and one that all tales agree on, is that the hoof-prints were preserved.

The witch's hut is believed to have been located under the present garage and the green in front of it, and where once there were eight holes in the ground marking the hoof prints caused by Byard's giant leaps, now two sets of four horseshoes mark the spots.

The present horseshoes were apparently installed in the late nineteenth century by Colonel Reeve of nearby Leadenham House who had the shoes, which collectively weighed nearly seven stone, set into large blocks of stone to prevent them being easily moved.

The sign board at the site gives the following interpretation:

This is the site of a famous Lincolnshire legend. The name Byards Leap derives from the name of the horse in the tale, he was a Bay horse called Bayard or Byard. The story has it that a Witch lived nearby and a villager from Ancaster was appointed to kill her. He used his horse Byard, he mounted the horse on the mounting stone by the farm gates on the other side of the now B6403. The horse took three huge leaps and the witch and the horse vanished. The horseshoes here and the other set in the small wood mark the horse's huge strides.

Shape-Shifting Witches

When two men were out shooting for game, they began to have problems with the gun whilst they were aiming at a hare. Finally, one of the men succeeded in shooting the hare in one of its legs just before it ran off out of sight.

As darkness fell, both men returned home for supper, but as the owner of the gun reached his mother's cottage he found that she was suffering with a pain in her leg. He fetched 'the oils' for her to rub on it and she went off to bed.

The next morning, the man was surprised to find that his mother wished to stay in bed. He was even more surprised when the old woman asked him to go to the 'wise man to find out what ails my leg, it is that bad, and what can I do to cure it.'

Though it was some distance to the wise man's house, the son did as he was asked. He was invited into the little back room and told to sit down. He then watched as the wise man randomly opened a big book, which looked very much like a family bible, sat on the table, and then went to a side cupboard, opened the door and looked inside, mumbling as he did so. The wise man then sat down in front of the big open book, which the man saw had strange marks and figures on it instead of words.

To his surprise, the man then saw a big bumblebee fly out of the cupboard and circle the room, buzzing very loudly as it did so. It then settled on one of the open pages of the big book, and the wise man looking closely at the bumblebee on the page and then scratched his chin and said, 'When did your mother first feel pain in her leg?'

'Last night,' replied the man, 'just before I came home for supper. She said it came on suddenly, cruel bad.'

'When did you shoot at that hare?' said the wise man.

The man was shocked that the wise man knew what he had been doing the night before, but replied truthfully, 'I didn't shoot at no hare.'

The wise man looked again at the book and said, 'No, I see you didn't, but it was shot with your gun, and in the left hind leg too.'

At this the man cried out in astonishment, 'Why, it is her left leg that is so cruel bad, the right ails nowt, and I remember it wor' the hare's left hind leg that was hit when my friend took my gun and fired because I could not get it to fire.'

'That must have been your guardian angel,' replied the wise man. 'It stopped the gun from going off in your hands when the hare was close, to prevent you from shooting your old mother, for she is always going about as a hare, witching folk. Why only a week or two ago I heard of her going out on the high road as a hare, in front of a team of horses, and frightening them so that they bolted and nearly overturned the wagon into the dyke. But her leg will soon mend, for all you have to do is to catch a hedgehog, saw of its left hind leg and give your mother to rub her bad leg with it.'

The son, grateful for the advice, thanked the wise man, paid him a crown and returned home. On the way he caught a hedgehog, sawed of its left leg, and gave it to his mother and told her how to use it. She rubbed her left leg with the hedgehog leg and very soon her own leg was better.

A similar story was recorded in Rowston, near Sleaford, of a witch who was peppered with shot while she was in the form of a hare, and returned to her cottage through the keyhole. She was found the next day, her body riddled with gunshot wounds.

Meg Wynne noted that the belief that women were able to take the shape of hares for disguise was still found in the Louth area in the 1970s. She looked even further back into history and discovered that a man named James Capp, of Cawthorpe, nar Bourne, was brought before the justices in 1660, fined for using a sling, filled with brimstone dust and lead, to kill a hare; he was warned that he might have killed a human being.

A sinister case of a shapeshifting woman was noted in *Lincolnshire Notes and Queries*, October 1891. It mentions Stainton, the wise man of Louth, of which more will be said later. I have, so far, made no progress in researching who the 'witch' and the victims were, and so I include the account exactly as recorded, in case others might like to carry out such research.

The Dream of H____ of Farforth

After his wife died, H____ of Farforth, near Tetford, became very depressed, and shutting himself up in one room at his house, drank heavily. While doing so he dreamed he was in hell, and that he saw his wife sitting in a magnificent armchair, and near to the chair were some devils who were busy making another like it. They told him that the chair was intended for him, and when it was finished they would come to fetch him and put him into it. This so terrified him that he gave up drinking and left Farforth, vowing he would never return. He died soon after, in London, and was brought back to be buried at Farforth by six black horses.

The Wise Men of Louth

At one time a young man from Sotby gradually got fatter and fatter, until he could barely walk. He thought he might be bewitched and went to see the wise man Stainton, of Louth, who said that a woman from his village had indeed bewitched him. Stainton offered to set the witch on fire. On returning home, the young man saw the old woman rushing out of her cottage in flames. She had been severely burned and almost died, but slowly recovered and lived for a few more years. However, her spell over the young man was broken and the man returned to his formerly thin self.

One day when someone was going to consult Stainton, they said to another, 'I wonder if the old devil will be in?' On reaching the wise man's house, they knocked on the door. Stainton opened it saying 'The old devil is in!'

Johnny o' the Grass, the wise man who was succeeded by Stainton, was once travelling on the road from Louth towards Wragby and Market Rasen, when he came to Tibs Tollbar, near Girsby Hall. He asked how much the toll fee would be and was told it was nothing for people, but it would cost so much for the donkey, because it isn't a person. Johnny got off his donkey and whispered something in its ear, and the donkey turned into a man. It followed Johnny past the tollbar, and a little further up the road Johnny stopped and waited for the donkey; he then whispered something into his ear again, and the donkey turned back into its natural form. The wise man then climbed onto his back and trotted off.

FIDDLER FYNES OF KIRKSTEAD

Fiddler Fynes was another wise man. He lived at Kirkstead and used a looking glass to find answers to people's questions. He considered himself a gentleman and he earned a living by playing the fiddle, alongside his wife who played the tambourine, at local celebrations. He also gained income by running a school at his house, which was situated on the opposite site of the road to Petwood. Fiddler was also a devout Christian who attended St Leonard's Church every Sunday.

One day, a local farmer was robbed and he sent for Fiddler Fynes to help him find the thief. Fiddler Fynes asked the man for a looking glass and told him that if the farmer looked into it, he would see the face of the thief. The farmer did this and saw the face of his farm hand. He was then told that if he broke the mirror, in the morning the thief would have a cut on his face in the same place that the mirror was broken. So, in the morning, after he had broken the mirror, the farmer confronted the young lad who had a cut on the side of his face, just as the Fiddler of Fynes had predicted. The farm hand was so scared that he confessed to his crime and returned the farmer's property, and the farmer forgave him.

THE WISE MAN OF LINCOLN

On a farm in Lincolnshire there had once been a great robbery, and nobody could find out who the thief was. At last the farmer's wife said to her husband, 'If you will send for the wise man of Lincoln, he will tell you.'

So the farmer did as his wife told him and sent for the wise man, who came in the form of a blackbird. As he flew into the farmyard, he frightened the cattle there so that a man who was threshing wheat in the barn could hardly keep them out.

Then the blackbird spoke to the farmer and said, 'Shall I bring the thieves into thy house, or make their shadows appear on the wall?'

The farmer answered, 'Do as thou think best.'

He had hardly spoken when one of the farmer's manservants, who had only that very moment begun his work in the fields, walked into the room and passed out.

When he had gone the blackbird said, 'That is one of them.'

Then he pointed to a shadow on the wall, and the farmer saw that it was the shadow of another of his servants.

'That is the other thief,' said the blackbird, and flew away.

Soon after, the two men were arrested and the money that they had stolen was found.

ST MARK'S EVE

St Mark's Eve (April 24th) used to be regarded as a very significant night for predicting the future. At many parishes around the country, including a number in Lincolnshire, the village seer (or wise woman or man) would watch the church between the hours of eleven and one. They would sit in silence waiting for the wraiths (spirits) of those who would die (and in some cases, those who would marry) during the following twelve-month period.

During the ritual, the wraiths of living members of the community would be seen by the observer as a procession, which typically went under the lychgate, through the church porch and then into the church. After a short time, the procession would reappear and disperse into the night. James Montgomery (1771–1854) included a compelling account of the ritual and its effects within his lengthy poem *The Vigil of St Mark*:

> Tis now, replied the village belle,
> St Mark's mysterious eve,
> And all that old traditions tell
> I tremblingly believe;
> How, when the midnight signal tolls,
> Along the churchyard green,
> A mournful train of sentenced souls
> In winding-sheets are seen.
> The ghosts of all whom death shall doom
> Within the coming year,
> In pale procession walk the gloom,
> Amid the silence drear.

The poem describes the horrific experience of an ordinary young man who tried the ritual. The historical record contains a number of true stories warning of the dangers of this, including two graphic accounts from Lincolnshire, both from the seventeenth century and both collected by the antiquarian Gervase Holles.

The first account was recorded in the early 1600s by Thomas Codd, Rector of Laceby, Lincolnshire, and a native of Haxey in the Isle of Axholme:

At Axholme, alias Haxey in the Isle, one Mr Edward Vicars (Curate to Mr William Dalby Vicar) together with one Robert Halywell a Tailor intending on St Mark's eve at night to watch in the Church-porch to see who should die in the year following (to this purpose using diverse Ceremonies) they addressing themselves to the business, Vicars (being then in his chamber) wished Halywell to be going before and he would presently follow him. Vicars fell asleep, and Halywell (attending his coming in the Church-porch) forthwith saw certain shapes presenting themselves to his view, resemblances (as he thought) of diverse of his neighbours ... and all of them died the year following; and Vicars himself (being asleep) his Phantasm was seen also, and died with the rest. This sight made Halywell so aghast that he looked like a Ghost ever since. The Lord Sheffield (hearing this relation) sent for Halywell to receive an account of it. The fellow fearing my Lord would cause him to watch the Church-porch again, hid himself in the Carrs, till he was almost starved. The number of those that died (whose Phantasmes Halywell saw) was as I take it about fourscore.

Hallywell may have believed, as many did within the area, that once a seer had carried out the church porch watch they would be expected to continue with it until they saw their own wraith. In other places it was believed that visions of wraiths would not appear until the vigil had been carried out for three years.

The second account is much more graphic, and was collected from the vicar of Grimsby, Livewell Rampayne, who had at the time of the incident been household chaplain to Sir Thomas Monson (or Munson) of Burton Hall about two miles north-west of Lincoln.

In the year 1631, two men (inhabitants of Burton) agreed betwixt themselves upon St Mark's eve at night to watch in the churchyard at Burton, to try whether or no (according to the ordinary belief amongst the common people) they should see the Spectra, or Phantasma of those persons which should die in that parish the year following. To this intent, having first performed the usual ceremonies and superstitions, late in the night, the moon shining then very bright, they repaired to the church porch, and there seated themselves, continuing there till near twelve of the clock. About which time (growing weary with expectation and partly with fear) they resolved to depart, but were held fast by a kind of insensible violence, not being able to move a foot.

About midnight, upon a sudden (as if the moon had been eclipsed), they were environed with a black darkness; immediately after, a kind of light, as if it had been a resultancy from torches. Then appears, coming towards the church porch, the minister of the place, with a book in his hand, and after him one in a winding-sheet, whom they both knew to resemble one of their neighbours. The church doors immediately fly open, and through pass the apparitions, and then the doors clap to again. Then they seem to hear a muttering, as if it were the burial service, with a rattling of bones and noise of earth, as in the filling up of a grave. Suddenly a still silence, and immediately after the apparition of the curate again, with another of their neighbours following in a winding-sheet, and so a third, fourth, and fifth, everyone attended with the same circumstances as the first.

These all having passed away, there ensued a serenity of the sky, the moon shining bright, as at the first; they themselves being restored to their former liberty to walk away, which they did sufficiently affrighted. The next day they kept within doors, and met not together, being both of them exceedingly ill, by reason of the affrightment which had terrified them the night before. Then they conferred their notes, and both of them could very well remember the circumstances of every passage. Three of the apparitions they well knew to resemble three of their neighbours; but the fourth (which seemed an infant), and the fifth (like an old man), they could not conceive any resemblance of. After this they confidently reported to everyone what they had done and seen; and in order designed to death those three of their neighbours, which came to pass accordingly.

Shortly after their deaths, a woman in the town was delivered of a child, which died likewise. So that now there wanted but one (the old man), to accomplish their predictions, which likewise came to pass after this manner. In that winter, about mid-January, began a sharp and long frost, during the continuance of which some of Sir John Munson's friends in Cheshire, having some occasion of intercourse with him, despatched away a foot messenger (an ancient man), with letters to him. This man, tramping this bitter weather over the mountains in Derbyshire, was nearly perished with cold, yet at last he arrived at Burton with his letters, where within a day or two he died. And these men, as soon as ever they see him, said peremptorily that he was the man whose apparition they see, and that doubtless he would die before he returned, which accordingly he did.

THE WEREWOLF OF LANGRICK FEN

In the 1920s, a young archaeologist by the name of Jones was digging in the peat bog at Langrick Fen when he found some apparently human bones. He took them back home and cleaned them up, and found to his horror that the bones made up a human skeleton but with a wolf's head. He was at a loss to understand how this could have come about and speculated that maybe it had been an exhibit from a travelling show – the bones of a half-man, half-wolf being.

That evening, as he continued to examine and ponder on the bones, he heard a scratching on the path outside and the sound of the latch being lifted on his locked door. He looked out the window and by the light of the moon he saw a strange dark figure with a human form and a wolf's head. The creature started to claw at the window and snarl at Jones, who ran to hide in the kitchen where he barricaded the door with furniture.

Jones heard the sound of breaking glass but then the snarling died down. He stayed in that kitchen all night,

not daring to sleep, and as dawn broke he crept out and over to the front door, wondering if the creature would still be there.

There was no sign of the creature, but there was glass all over the floor by the window, and the table on which the bones had been placed had been overturned. Jones knew that there was only one thing he should do with the bones.

He hastily gathered all the bones together, placed them into a box and put the box into a bag, which he buried deep in the peat bog where he had found them. He returned home and was never again disturbed by the supernatural visitor.

People said that for many years after, the man would tell his tale to those who would listen, and as he recounted the happenings of the night the tremor could still be heard in his voice and the fear still seen in his eyes.

Christopher Marlowe wrote an account of the mystery from Langrick Fen, in his *Legends of the Fenland People*. A variant of the 'true' story was also told by Ethel Rudkin to a neighbour in Spilsby in the 1970s. I have combined the two narratives.

Langrick (or Langriville / Langrickville) is a small village in East Lindsey, five miles north-west of Boston. The land was once part of Wildmore Fen, and the village did not come into existence until the land had been successfully drained and enclosed in 1812.

6

OF PEOPLE
AND PLACES

This section is made up of a diverse set of tales about people in Lincolnshire. The first is the true story of 'Ten-Pint Smith of Louth', a popular tale that has been researched by a local historian. This will be followed by an entertaining tale from the seventeenth-century diarist Abraham de la Pryme, concerning the Lacy family of Winterton, and a not dissimilar tale from the Tattershall area.

A Lincolnshire version of a traditional tale, of a type that is found elsewhere around the country, will follow along with the true account of sacrilege in the church at Holbeach, over two hundred years ago.

TEN-PINT SMITH OF LOUTH

It is said that there once lived in the Lincolnshire market town of Louth, a man who had been given the nickname of 'Six-Pint Smith'. He was so known, due to his ability to drink half a pint of beer for each stroke of the church clock at midday.

One day, Six-Pint Smith was at Louth Fair when he met a pedlar who, on hearing of his reputation, challenged him to a drinking contest. Smith drank from a quart mug but the pedlar drank twice as much, as he had a quart mug in each hand. After Smith had drunk eight pints, the pedlar offered to give him all his goods if he would down two more pints and then climb the church steeple. Smith accepted the challenge and then handed the pedlar his tailcoat whilst he started his climb.

On reaching the top of the spire, which is nearly 300ft high, Smith took off his kerchief and tied it around the iron which supported the weathercock. He then remained on the top stone and danced a hornpipe to a gradually increasing crowd of onlookers. He then began his descent, and part way down he paused to stand on one leg with arms outstretched on the point of one of the pinnacles.

When Smith reached the ground he found that the pedlar had disappeared with his tailcoat, which had his purse of money in the pocket. He had to pay for all the beer they had consumed and get used to his new nickname of 'Ten-Pint Smith'.

This tale featured in the 'Intelligence from various Parts of the Country' column of *The Gentleman's Magazine*, 1818, as follows:

> A man of the name of Smith lately had the temerity, after drinking about ten pints of ale, to ascend the spire of Louth church, which is nearly 300 feet high, and tie a handkerchief round the iron which supports the weathercock; after he had remained some time upon the top stone, danced a hornpipe, and performed several antics, he descended with all the composure imaginable to the bottom of the spire, and on the point of one of the pinnacles of the tower he stood upon one leg, with his arms extended, and made his congre to the numerous spectators below, who witnessed this piece of presumption with horror and astonishment.

The Louth historian, David Robinson OBE, who carried out extensive research and wrote a number of books on the town, gave the date for the event as 5 May 1818. He also discovered that the full name and occupation of the climber was Benjamin Smith, a cobbler. Robinson also noted that there had been a previous unauthorised ascent and descent of the spire on 22 November 1771, by Anthony Fountain, a sailor from Doncaster.

Whatever the date, the background and the actual events of the day, St James' Church in Westgate, Louth, has the tallest spire, at 295ft, of any Anglican parish church in England.

THE UNGRATEFUL SONS

In Winterton there once lived a Mr Lacy who, when he grew very old, left all he had to his three sons, on condition that one should keep him one week, the second on the next and so on.

It so happened that it did not take long for the sons to grow tired of him, for they had all they wanted, and now saw their father as little more than a dog that needed feeding and caring for. The old man, seeing how things had changed and feeling slighted, went to see a friend who was a lawyer to ask for advice. The lawyer told him that sadly no law in the land could help him nor yield him any comfort. The old man looked so downhearted that the lawyer thought for a moment, and then said, 'I have an idea for something you can do, if you will just agree to do exactly as I say, I will help you.'

Mr Lacy was exceedingly glad. 'For God's sake tell me what I should do, for I am tired and hungry and will do anything to change the way that I have to live at the moment.'

'Well,' says the lawyer, 'you have been a great friend of mine in my need, and I will now be one to you in your need. I will lend you a strong box with a strong lock on it, in which shall be contained £1,000; you shall pretend to have fetched it from me, as though I had looked after it for you. Each week when you go to each of your sons' houses, you will make it your business to be always counting the money, and rattling it about, and you shall see that, for the love of it, they'll soon love you again, and make very much of you, and maintain you joyfully, willingly, and plentifully, unto your dying day.'

The old man thanked the lawyer for this good advice and kind offer, and returned to see him a few days later to collect the box full of money. He took it to each of his sons' houses in turn and, as advised, made a big fuss of counting his money. At this, his sons soon fell in love with him again and cared for him well. When he was convinced that their love for him continued steadfast and firm, he took the strong box out of the house and returned it to the lawyer, thanking him exceedingly for his help.

When he returned to his sons, he made them believe that he had hidden the box again, and that he would give it to the one who he loved best when he died. This made them all so observant of him that he lived the rest of his days in great peace and happiness amongst them, and died full of years.

However, he made sure that before he died he upbraided them for their former ingratitude, told them the whole history of the box, and forgave them.

COUGH IN THE KITCHEN

There once was a farmer who lived near Tattershall, who was a self-made man, and his manners reflected this. He had two big farms and worked over 1,000 acres in total, with the help of his only son. He also had a daughter, who had scorned the rich old man her father had chosen for her, and married beneath her status.

When the man's wife died the son returned home to look after his father, bringing his new wife with him.

This young woman was quite the 'lady' and wanted to ensure the fortune of herself and her husband, and she persuaded her husband to say to his father, 'As you are getting old and soon will not be able to go about the farm in the way you had before, perhaps it might be best to make over the farm to us and we can see that you are well fed and looked after so that you can relax in your old age.'

The farmer agreed to this and, neglecting his daughter, asked a solicitor to help him write his will to leave everything to his son. He gave this new will to his son and the wife put it away for safekeeping.

As soon as this was done, the son's wife started to make things very unpleasant for him. She was rude to his friends and discouraged them from visiting him. Along with this, more and more genteel people would call round, snubbing the coarse old man, so much so that he would take himself off to the kitchen.

One evening, as the old man sat by the fire in the parlour warming himself, as he had a nasty cough and cold, a very grand group of visitors arrived. This group of well-dressed strangers ignored the old man completely until he started to cough, and then his son said to him, 'You had best go cough in the kitchen.'

The poor old man went to sit on the kitchen settle and did a bit of thinking, along with the coughing, before retiring to bed. He thought about his old wife and how their son was ashamed of him and he decided that things must change.

In the morning he was late getting up and his son had gone about his business. He said to his daughter-in-law, 'I was thinking last night that I had forgotten to put a piece of land in the will. Can you get it for me so that I can check?'

The woman then went away and returned with the document, which the old man slowly read, as his eyes were not so good, and he had not been good at learning. His daughter-in-law soon grew tired of waiting and went off, saying that she would be back in a minute.

As soon as she was out of the room, the old man tore up the will and threw the pieces onto the fire. When the woman returned she asked, 'Where is the will? Have you finished with it? Did you find out if you had missed a piece of land from it?'

The old man replied, 'Yes I have finished with it. The will is in the fire. I am going to make a new will and I shall include all my land on it, but it won't be for you and my selfish son. I shall leave everything to my daughter. I am going to ask her to come and live with me, and you and your husband can go and cough in the kitchen, but not this one!'

The Lass That Saw Her Own Grave Dug

Did I ever tell ye about our Bessie, that saw her own grave dug, poor lass? It's a queer tale that, and every word of it's true. She was a real pretty lass, with flaxen hair and blue eyes, and there was a man called Fox, that was strange and fond of her.

Well, he made a deal of her, and when he'd got his own work done, he'd tidy himself up a bit and then walk over to her father's house, to help her the milk cows, serve the pigs, and such like.

Folks reckoned he was clear soft about the lass, but the girl's father hated to see him lounging about the place, and always said, 'He's over keen by half, and you know, when love's over strong it never lasts long.'

However, nobody but the old women took any notice of him. Everybody knew that he thought the lass could have got her work done without any of Fox's help, and get through it a lot quicker an' all, and so folks only laughed when he carried on.

Well, one day, when her father was out singling turnips, Fox came over and said, 'I've got to go to market to-morrow. If you can, come to the big ash in Galley-dales, and then I can see you home, and we'll sort out about getting married.'

'That's a long way to walk,' says the lass, 'and it's a strange lonely road, and I should scare if I met anything.'

But at last Fox persuaded her and she said she would be under the ash a bit after seven, and then off he went. Well, that night the lass had a strange queer dream, and she said to herself the next day, 'I hadn't that there dream for nowt. I'll be in Galley-dales before he gets there, I reckon; then I shall get to know what he's up to.'

So she gets her work done, and then she
sets off to Galley-dales without saying nowt
to nobody. And when she gets to the big
ash tree, she climbs up and hides herself
in the boughs, sitting as still as a bee.

After a while, Fox comes along,
pulls a spade out of the hedge bottom
and begins to dig a grave beneath the
ash. He was that busy with it that
he never looked up and saw the lass.
After he'd got it done, he walked up
and down, smoking and looking at
the grave and talking to himself.

He waited and waited for the lass
until he was tired but she never came,
and at last he shovelled the earth into
the grave again and went away, chunter-
ing. Then the lass slipped down from
the tree and ran home, as quick as
if a boggart was after her. And the next day,
when Fox came and asked why she'd stood him up, she
says that she'll tell him if he can solve this riddle:

> Riddle me, riddle me righ,
> Up in the boughs so high;
> The wind it blew,
> The cocks they crew,
> The leaves did shake,
> My heart did ache
> To see the hole
> The fox did make;
> Riddle me, riddle me righ.

And when Fox heard this he was about to run off, but in came the lass' father, with five or six other men, and they took him straight away to prison. And if it hadn't been for that there dream that was sent her, the lass would have been murdered, as true as I stand here.

Mabel Peacock included the story in her *Tales and Rhymes in Lindsey Folk-Speech*. In her unpublished notes, Mabel recorded that she was also told the story in 1895 by some-one with the initials R.G.N., who said it was related to him by his foreman. This narrator said that the story was set in Buslingthorpe, that the girl in the story was later known as 'Mrs C.', and that she was considered 'a queer woman'. He added that 'the grave is to be seen there yet'. I have been unable to trace the location of 'Galley-dales' as mentioned in the text, or find a female that I could con-firm as Mrs C.

Ken Pearson recorded a similar story and noted its appearance in different forms at different locations (he set his meeting at Paddy Lane Crossroads but he did not specify where this was, or even if it was in Lincolnshire). Mabel Peacock also acknowledged the story as a fragment of an old folk tale that is found in many places, including Yorkshire, Derbyshire, Cambridgeshire, Buckinghamshire, Gloucestershire, Oxfordshire, Cornwall and in America. The story is similar to the tale of 'Mr Fox's Courtship', 'The Girl Who Got Up the Tree' and 'The Oxford Student' – the former, and other variants, contain similar riddles.

THE HOLBEACH GAMESTERS

At the 'Chequers' long famed to quaff then did delight
The Burghers both ancient and young.
With smoking and cards, passed the dull winter night.
They joked and they laughed and they sung.

Three revellers left, when the midnight was come.
Unable their game to pursue.
Repaired, most unhallowed, to visit the tomb
Where enshrouded lay one of their crew.

For he, late-departed, renowned was at whist.
The marsh-men still tell of his fame,
Till Death with a spade struck the cards from his fist
And spoiled both his hand and his game.

The above verses, from a poem by Thomas Hardwicke Rawnsley (1789–1861) of Bourne, were written down in about the year 1800. They describe an incident that took place in Holbeach in 1783 during which Holbeach All Saints Church was desecrated by the actions of a band of card players. This sounds like just a story but it is actually based around fact, and for at least a hundred years was something that many local people did not want to talk about.

In the year 1783, a group of three men were drinking, smoking and playing cards at The Chequers Hotel. As they played Long Whist, they talked of a dear friend who had recently died and who had played regularly with them.

As they left The Chequers their thoughts were still with their departed friend, and they reasoned that it must be dull for him beneath the earth in his newly filled grave.

With the drink affecting their judgement, they decided that they would disinter their friend and have one last game with him, to cheer him up.

They fetched spades and picks, and by the light of the moon, dug up their friend. They then carried his corpse through the big oak door and into the church. Down the nave they walked and into the chancel, where they cleared the high altar of all except the candles. They then propped up their dead friend and by candlelight played their preferred game, with their friend as the holder of the dummy hand.

But outside of the church, a man saw the flickering of the candles and fetched a ladder. Peeking through the window, he saw the corpse with the cards in its hand and ran to raise the alarm. Soon a group of men from The Chequers were stomping up the path to the church porch. As they gripped the handle of the big oak door the mood inside the church changed.

Those gamesters suddenly saw clearly what they had done and ran to escape, meeting the others on the way. Soon they were filled with remorse. They laid their friend to rest once again and tried to return to their former lives.

The local newspaper mentioned nothing of the events of that night but the local people retained the memories and the scornful attitude. Twenty years later, one of the gamesters, a doctor, cut his arms and bled to death. As it was a suicide, he was buried not in the churchyard but at a spot off the Spalding Road, a mile away.

Over a century later, research recovered from the oral testimonies of elderly people who had been told the truth of the terrible secrets by their long-dead parents revealed the name of the doctor to be Jonathan Watson. His companions were John Key, William Slator and a man named Wheldale.

Another version of the tale has the men playing cards with the body of a woman who had been laid on the communion table in preparation for burial the following day; another described their friend as in a similar position awaiting burial after dying during a previous game; and a third version tells how a phantom appeared in the church and the men were taken by the Devil.

The latter version was recounted by a former vicar of All Saints Church to Ethel Rudkin in 1931. His graphic account had the dummy slip between the table and the wall and a fiend appear in his place saying in a sepulchral voice: 'Both the game and the gamesters are lost!' The fiend then disappeared and they propped the corpse up again and continued playing, determined to finish the game. They played for some time but the dummy and his partner kept winning, until the dummy slipped down again, and this time three fiends appeared and carried the players off in 'a cloud of foul smelling sulphur'.

The historical record, as recounted by Grant MacDonald, the vicar of St Mark's in Holbeach in 1890, reveals that the men paid for damage to the tomb and also shows that a century after the sacrilege, a Holbeach man who had died elsewhere was laid out overnight in the church. An elaborate all-night vigil was held by the residents of the town, perhaps to atone for the wickedness of the ancestors, or maybe to guard against the sacrilegious happenings occurring again!

Whatever the situation, Ethel Rudkin was informed that there were great problems getting Holbeach parishioners to attend services after dusk on account of the 'haunting' there. Mrs Bond, wife of a former vicar of Holbeach, told Ethel that, 'No one would enter the church alone at night on any account in case they should see the game of cards going on the high altar with a corpse as dummy.'

7

OF KINGS
AND MONKS
AND HERMITS

This section contains three ancient tales that may be regarded more as histories than folk tales; the other parts are from the folk stories that have grown around the histories, combined with factual details of dates and places, where these are known. The first tale is about St Guthlac and Crowland Abbey, a tale that begins much like that of William of Lindholme but the hermits life was so venerated that an abbey was built in his memory.

The second tale follows on from the old tradition that the town of Grimsby was founded by a Danish fisherman. This same fisherman played an integral part in the story of 'Havelok the Dane'. I have adapted Mabel Peacock's version, which was based on a manuscript in the Laudian collection of the Bodleian Library.

The story of Havelok is followed by a tale that overturns the conventional story (or history) which states that, after King John lost his jewels when his baggage train was sucked into the quicksand of the Wash, he died at Newark Castle from dysentery brought on by over-indulgence.

The final tale in this section is a version of the traditional folk tale 'Cinderella', collected by Marie Balfour. It is not a history, nor does it mention any places in Lincolnshire, however, it was collected in the county, and according to the notes in Joseph Jacobs' *More English Fairy Tales*, it was originally told in dialect. Sadly this was removed.

St Guthlac and Crowland Abbey

Standing tall above the edge of Deeping Fen, close to the Lincolnshire border with Peterborough and Cambridgeshire, are the spectacular ruins of the abbey of Crowland. Known until the late medieval era as Croyland, the abbey was once on an island surrounded by vast swamp-land, reachable only by boat.

John Clare described the ruins he found when he visited Crowland Abbey in 1826/27:

> In sooth, it seems right awful and sublime
> To gaze by moonlight on the shattered pile
> Of this old Abbey, struggling still with Time –
> The grey owl hooting from its rents the while;
> And tottering stones, as wakened by the sound,
> Crumbling from arch and battlement around,
> Urging dread echoes from the gloomy aisle,
> To sink more silent still. The very ground
> In Desolation's garment doth appear,
> The lapse of age and mystery profound.

> We gaze on wrecks of ornamented stones,
>
> On tombs whose sculptures half erased appear,
>
> On rank weeds, battening over human bones,
>
> Till even one's very shadow seems to fear.

Guthlac was born in about the year AD 673, the son of a Mercian nobleman. It was said that in boyhood he showed extraordinary signs of piety, but despite this he took up a profitable career as a soldier for eight or nine years. He then became filled with remorse and decided, at the age of twenty-four, to become a monk at the abbey in Repton, Derbyshire. However, two years after taking his vows, he decided that the monastic life was too comfortable and became committed to following Christ's example, by retreating to the 'wilderness'. He would, he decided, become a hermit in one of the most inhospitable places in the land of the Middle Angles, the mosquito-infested Fens.

When Guthlac arrived on the island of Croyland he found it to be a very wild inhospitable place, covered in sedgy marshes, woods and pools. He constructed a small cell in a plundered bronze-age barrow and prepared to live the remainder of his life in solitude, but soon found that there were other inhabitants on the island, hobgoblins or demon creatures (who spoke the ancient language of the British, similar to Welsh) would descend on him in his cell, drag him out and sometimes even throw him in the air, or into the bogs, or through the brambles. Felix, in his *Life of Saint Guthlac*, described the demons:

> They were ferocious in appearance, terrible in shape with great heads, long necks, thin faces, yellow complexions, filthy

beards, shaggy ears, wild foreheads, fierce eyes, foul mouths, horses' teeth, throats vomiting flames, twisted jaws, thick lips, strident voices, singed hair, fat cheeks, pigeons breasts, scabby thighs, knotty knees, crooked legs, swollen ankles, splay feet, spreading mouths, raucous cries. For they grew so terrible to hear with their mighty shriekings that they filled almost the whole intervening space between earth and heaven with their discordant bellowings.

Guthlac did not let the actions of the demons deter him from his life of penance and, as well as contracting ague, and suffering from malnutrition, he soon became friends with the birds and fishes. He wore neither wool nor linen garments, nor any other soft material, and made his clothes from animal skins. He would eat no food until sundown and then only a scrap of barley bread and a cup of water. His piety gained him fame and many pilgrims came to visit him in his 'cell', including Aethelbald, who was later to become king, and would help to fund a chapel at Croyland.

During Holy Week in the year 714 Guthlac became ill and predicted his own death to be seven days later. He died joyfully on 11 April and, at his request, his funeral rites were performed by his sister, Pega. His burial place soon became a place of miracles, and a year later his sister had his body exhumed and moved to the newly founded Benedictine monastery. They found his shroud shining with light and his body incorrupt.

Pega lived a day away from Croyland by boat, in a cell on the site of what is now known as the village of Peakirk in Cambridgeshire. After her brother's death she went on a pilgrimage to Rome, where she died in 719.

In the ninth century, at the time of the Viking raids, standing high on a hill overlooking the fenland waterways Croyland Monastery was an easy target for these master mariners. They sailed their narrow longboats up to the abbey, ransacked the place, and killed many of the monks, including the Abbot Theodore. In 947, the abbey was rebuilt and dedicated to St Mary the Virgin, St Bartholomew and St Guthlac.

Later, when King John was travelling around the land collecting his treasures and punishing the rebellious barons, he sent his mercenary captain, Saveric de Mauleon, to Croyland, where he believed some of the rebels were hiding. Armed men rode into the cloisters, the monastic buildings and the church while mass was being celebrated. Finding none of the rebels they were searching for, they dragged men away from the altar and carried them off as prisoners. They also set fire to the abbey and the harvest, and seized sheep and cattle as booty.

At the time of the Dissolution of the Monasteries in 1539 the eastern parts of the abbey church and the monastic buildings were again subject to destruction, though the nave and aisles were retained for use by the parish. After being further damaged by Parliamentarian forces during the English Civil War in 1643, the nave roof fell in 1720 and the main south wall was demolished in 1744. This left the outer north aisle, which is still in use as the parish church today.

About a mile away from the abbey, along Wash Bank, can be found St Guthlac's Cross from the thirteenth century, which marks the boundary of the former Abbey Lands. The Latin inscription on the cross, which used to be clearly visible, can be translated as, 'This stone, I say, is Guthlac's utmost bound.'

An effigy of Guthlac can be found in St Guthlac's Church in Market Deeping. He is also depicted in two stained-glass windows on the south side of the church; one Victorian and the other Edwardian.

The skull of Abbot Theodore used to be on display in the church until it was stolen in 1982. It was returned anonymously in 1999.

HAVELOK, GOLDBOROUGH AND GRIM

Goldborough, the daughter of King Athelwold, was very young when her father died. Too young, in fact, to walk or speak. Before his death at Winchester, her father had commanded his earls and barons to attend on him, and he declared that Earl Godrich of Cornwall should guard his daughter until she was old enough to wed the fairest and strongest man alive. She would then rule with her husband's assistance, he said.

The King, satisfied that he had left his kingdom safe for his daughter, was shriven, took the sacrament, and then passed away. A short time afterwards, Earl Godrich put the knights he most trusted into the castles and made all the people swear to be true to him until the maiden was twenty years old.

Goldborough grew into the fairest of women and Earl Godrich, seeing how wise, chaste and fair she was, thought to himself, 'Shall she be Queen and Lady over me? Shall I yield England to a girl? I have a son, a full fair lad, he shall have all England.'

Godrich then disregarded his oath and sent the maiden to Dover, where he imprisoned her and though he clothed and fed her, he did so without kindness and denied her visits from her friends.

In Denmark at the time, the king was named Birkabeyn. He was a strong and just man and skilled at arms. He was also a good and loving father to his son and two daughters. But death came upon him whilst he was still in his prime and whilst he lay with his strength ebbing away, he called his friend Godard to him and said, 'Here I deliver thee my three children and all Denmark, till my son be of age, and I will have thee swear that thou wilt care for my children till my son is a knight, and then give him his kingdom and all that belongs to it.'

Godard swore to do as Birkabeyn wished, and he and all the Danish knights wept as the great king died and was laid in his grave. Godard then took the Prince Havelok and his sisters Swanborough and Helfled and shut them up in a castle, denying their kin access. He kept the children scantily clad and sore for hunger and cold.

One day, Godard came to the tower where the children were imprisoned and he cut the throats of the two young maidens. He then turned to their brother, but Havelok said to him, 'Lord, have mercy now. I will give you all of Denmark, and I will swear Birkabeyn never got me if you will let me go. I will sail far from here and never return.'

Godard, on hearing this, felt some guilt for what he had done, but as he feared for his future and his power he decided to put the boy to sea, so that he will be as dead. He sent for a fisherman named Grim and said that he would make him rich if he would throw the ragged looking boy into the sea. Grim agreed to carry out the task and bound and gagged the boy, put him in a sack and carried him home. He told his wife of their good fortune and asked her to tend and care for the boy, but to keep him bound and gagged at all times.

At midnight, Grim went to pick up the young boy to take him to the sea as requested by Godard. But as he did so, he noticed a bright light around the child. He then saw, on the boys right shoulder, a king's mark – a cross of red gold, bright and fair. He realised that he must be Havelok, the heir to the throne, who none had seen for some time, and changed his mind about obeying his order. 'Lord, have mercy on us,' he said, 'we will feed thee well till thou can bear helm, shield and spear; and Godard, the traitor, shall never know. We will serve thee faithfully until thou grants us freedom.'

Grim then fed the boy, made him comfortable, and gave him a bed to sleep in soundly. The next morning, Grim went to see Godard and said, 'Lord, I have done your bidding. The lad lies drowned in the sea. Now make me free with thy charter?'

But Godard looked at him and said, 'Wilt thou now be an Earl? Go home churl and remain a bondsman, for thou has done a foul deed for which I could have thee led to the gallows.'

Grim then realised that he must take Havelok away to save both their lives. He sold all he possessed and fitted out a ship. He then took Havelok, along with his own wife, three sons and two daughters, out onto the high sea.

The wind blew the ship to England and they landed in the Humber, where they built an earthen house and so established the place known as Grimsby.

Grim was a good fisher and took many a fish with hook and net. He made panniers for himself and his sons to take the catch to trade in the towns and farmsteads of Lindsey, and they never returned home with empty hands. For twelve winters they worked before Havelok joined them in their trade.

Soon after this, a great famine came upon the land and with this the catches of fish grew less. Grim knew not how he could feed his family and Havelok, and for fear that they would all die of hunger he sent Havelok to Lincoln. He made him a coat from his sail but could provide the young man with neither hose nor shoes for his feet.

When Havelok arrived in Lincoln City he could find no work for two days. But on the third day he heard a call for porters and he rushed forth. The task was to carry meat to the castle, and for this he was given a farthing cake. The next day he sat waiting for the earl's cook so that he could once again carry the meat for the castle.

His keenness was soon rewarded and the cook gave him a job in the kitchen, where he worked well and soon came to be regarded as the hardest of workers and the gentlest of men. The cook also brought him some clothes and without his old coat, everyone could see he was as handsome as a king and taller by the shoulders than the tallest of other men.

It so happened that one day Earl Godrich came to Lincoln to hold a parliament, and with him came all the young knights. They held a contest in which all were challenged to lift and throw a large stone. Most could barely lift this stone but Havelok, when urged on by his master the cook, lifted it and flung it more than 12ft.

Havelok's reputation soon spread and reached the ears of Godrich who reasoned that, as King Athelwold had said that he should give Goldborough the best and strongest man alive for a husband, Havelok could be such a man, and easy to control, as he was only a bondsman's son.

So Godrich sent for Goldborough and told her of his plans, but she said that she would marry none but a king's son. This angered the earl who said that she would marry the cook's lad, and it would be on the morrow. He then called for Havelok and asked if he would take a wife. Havelok responded by saying, 'Nay, what should I do with a wife? I have nothing to offer her.'

Godrich was furious at this and threatened that if Havelok did not marry Goldborough he would hang him high or put out his eyes. To Goldborough he said that if she did not wed, he would send her to the gallows or have her burnt in fire. And so the couple were married.

When Havelok was first given time alone with his new wife he persuaded her that they must flee as Godrich hated them so much. They set off for Grimsby to see Grim and his three sons.

When they arrived they found that Grim had died, but his children were pleased to see them and made them welcome. That night, in their bed, Goldborough lay sorrowfully, believing she had betrayed her father in marrying one so lowly. But as darkness fell she saw light shine from the mouth of the sleeping Havelok and she saw the noble cross of red gold on his shoulder.

She then heard the voice of an angel saying that, 'Havelok is heir of a king. He shall have Denmark and England, and thou shalt be Queen.'

That night, Havelok dreamed of Denmark, and in the morning he told his wife of his desire to return to the land of his birth. She bade him prepare a ship for sail, and Grim's sons, Robert the Red, William Wenduth and Hugh Raven, offered to travel with them.

They set sail and the crossing was calm. They soon arrived in Denmark and, dressed as merchants, they were made welcome by the local landowner Earl Ubbe. Havelok had many adventures and proved to be strong, brave and fearless. It was not long before the light that shone from him whilst he was asleep, and the kingly mark on his shoulder, was observed. Havelok was recognised as the son of Birkabeyn, and people were reminded of the treachery of Godard, of the murder of Havelok's sisters, and how the boy was borne over the sea by Grim, who fed and fostered him in England. Everyone agreed 'that there was no knight half so brave in this middle earth'.

Ubbe then dubbed Havelok, Robert, William and Hugh knights and also made Havelok king. With 100 other knights and 5,000 men they swore on the book and the altar that they would not rest until they had brought Godard to justice.

Godard was confronted and a great battle took place in which all his men were slain, and the traitor was bound and gagged and brought before Havelok. It was then agreed by all present that Godard be shriven, flayed and the hanged for his treason.

Havelok then gave all that he had gained to the care of Ubbe and set sail back to Grimsby to make a priory of Black Monks and to thank God for his good fortune.

But when Godrich heard that Havelok had been made King of Denmark, he realised the he would soon wish to gain England by right of his marriage to Goldborough. He soon raised an army and marched north. The two armies met at a place near Grimsby and a great battle took place. Thousands of knights were slain on each side, and eventually Godrich was wounded and captured and tried for his traitorous deeds. He was judged guilty and taken to Lincoln, where he was bound to a stake and burnt to dust.

Havelok then gained the surety of all the English and the celebrations for his coronation lasted for forty days. During this time he rewarded the cook by giving him an Earldom and the hand of one of the daughters of Grim in marriage. He also rewarded all the others that had helped him, and gave Ubbe the governance of Denmark in his stead.

Havelok and Goldborough reigned for sixty years and had fifteen sons and daughters, all of whom became kings and queens.

The seal of the Corporation of Great Grimsby, which is believed to date back to the time of King Edward I (1272–1307), depicts Gryem (Grim) the warrior as the central character, wielding a drawn sword and holding a shield, with Habloc (Havelok) at his right hand and Goldebvgh (Goldborough) at his left, both with crowns above their heads. An enlarged version of the medieval seal can be found on the wall of the Central Library, near the entrance.

A statue of Grim and Havelok was installed outside the Grimsby Institute at Nuns Corner in 1973, but was removed in 2006 after it was decapitated by vandals.

According to legend, the stone thrown by Havelok used to be accessible to visitors in Lincoln, but it's whereabouts are now unknown. Holles reported in 1630 that there used to be 'a great blew Boundry-Stone lying at ye East-End of Briggowgate, which retaines ye name of Hauelocks-Stone to this day'.

King John and Brother Simon

In the autumn of 1216, King John criss-crossed the country, collecting royal treasure that had been left for safekeeping in the hands of the Knights Templar, Knights Hospitaller and various religious houses. Since being forced to sign the Magna Carta a year earlier, he no longer trusted the barons. He wanted his treasure close by him, and besides, he needed to pay for the loyalty of the 2,000 mounted knights and their retainers who travelled with him.

Now he travelled with the royal regalia and crown jewels, some dating back to the time of King Alfred, many of which were passed to him by his grandmother, the Empress Matilda. Each time he stopped overnight, he examined the beauty of the great crowns, the sceptres and gold wands, along with the many precious jewels, rings and amulets.

Thirteenth-century historian Matthew Paris recorded how, in late September, King John and his mercenaries had chased rebel barons into the Isle of Axholme, by way of Barton, Scotter and Stowe. He ravaged the isle with fire and sword and then continued around the county:

> From Lincoln northward to Grimsby, and thence south again to Spalding, the Lincolnshire fields – how, at the beginning of October, all white to harvest – were given to the flames, and the houses and farm buildings sacked and destroyed by the terrible host with the King at its head, looting and destroying the estates of disloyal barons at Grimsby, Louth and Spalding.

The King then crossed the Wash to Lynn in Norfolk, to spend a few days surrounded by loyal followers.

On 12 October he left Lynn to return to Lincolnshire, this time to St Mary's Abbey, Swineshead, stopping overnight at Wisbech in Cambridgeshire. When he reached his final destination he heard that his baggage train had been overtaken by the tide whilst trying to cross the Wellstream and it was reported to him that many of his possessions and men had perished.

At the abbey he sought to drown his sorrows with wine and women. In this house of God the wine was available in plenty but the only woman worth attention was the fair Judith, the sister of William the Abbot.

Judith, a beautiful young woman, was appalled when King John commanded that she attend him in his chamber, and so were the monks within the Abbey.

One of their number, Brother Simon, asked to speak privately to William the Abbot and asked to be granted absolution for what he was about to do. Satisfied that his sins would be forgiven, the young monk mixed poison with some new cider.

He then took the deadly concoction to the King's chamber and knocked on the door. On being allowed into the room he saw the beautiful Judith kneeling at the King's feet in a state of fear and the king in a state of intoxication, stroking her hair.

'For what do we owe this intrusion, sir monk?' asked the King.

Brother Simon held out the jug of cider and a tankard and explained that the Abbots would like the King to taste the new cider brewed in the Abbey from apples grown in their own orchards.

The King replied, 'It must be special indeed, to merit such an intrusion upon the King's privacy. Drink first, sir monk that I might have assurance that it is indeed a special brew.'

The young monk took a large sip of the cider and the King followed suit, and soon the jug was empty. The monk took his leave and the King returned his attention to Judith.

But as soon as his hand ventured lower than to stroke her beautiful hair his stomach was gripped by deadly pains and he rushed to the garde-robe where his 'bowels burst out.'

For the next five days, as the King continued his journey, he suffered from what he and his retainers believed to be dysentery. Unable to ride, he was carried in a litter, stopping frequently when the pains became unbearable.

Brother Simon, similarly afflicted, was cared for secretly within the abbey walls.

After stopping overnight at Lafford Castle (Sleaford) and Hough-on-the-Hill, the royal retinue reached Newark. The King died in the early hours of 19th October, and was buried in Worcester Cathedral wearing a cloak given to him by Abbot Croxton, who had given him the last rites and had then returned to prepare the body for burial.

Immediately upon his death, the King's body was stripped of everything except his undergarments. His apartments were ransacked and it was said that 'wayfarers on the roads around Newark reported men and laden packhorse's leaving the city'.

But what is the truth behind this story?

Between 3 and 9 October, King John was travelling around Lincolnshire causing trouble to those disloyal to him. He was also very unpopular with Cistercian religious houses, such as Swineshead.

The King also stayed at Lynn in Norfolk before travelling, via Wisbech and Swineshead, to Newark, and there were a number of contemporary reports of his baggage train being lost. Shakespeare referred to the poisoning legend, and an eighteenth-century map of the area names Swineshead as 'the Abbey where King John sickened'.

Did the retainers really steal the clothes off King John's back? And did he really lose his treasure in the Wash? Of the latter it has not been proven either way. Some argue that the King would never have let his treasure out of his sight and so it could not have been lost in the crossing. Others are still looking for the treasure.

In 1797, an exhumation of the corpse in Worcester Cathedral showed the skeleton of the King wrapped in a monk's cowl. His nine-year-old son Henry was crowned with just a simple gold band. Some of the recorded crown jewels did reappear, but many were never seen again.

Richard Waters, an amateur historian with a keen interest in folklore, produced a very informative little booklet on all the controversies surrounding the death of King John. He also notes that an effigy from Brother Simon's tomb survives at Swineshead, and depicts the monk as a Knight's Templar!

Sadly, the owner of the property on which the effigy of Brother Simon can be seen prefers to keep their anonymity. With regard to Swineshead Abbey, it only survives as a series of buried remains and earthwork features partly overlain by Abbey Farm, about half a mile north-east of the town.

TATTERCOATS

In a great palace by the sea there once dwelt a very rich old lord, who had neither wife nor children living, only one little granddaughter whose face he had never seen in all her life. His favourite daughter died giving birth to her, and he hated her bitterly because of this. When the old nurse brought him the baby he swore that it might live or die as it liked, but he would never look on its face as long as it lived.

So he turned his back and sat by his window looking out over the sea, weeping great tears for his lost daughter, till his white hair and beard grew down over his shoulders and twined round his chair and crept into the chinks of the floor; and his tears, dropping onto the window ledge, wore a channel through the stone and ran away in a little river to the great sea.

Meanwhile, his granddaughter grew up with no one to care for her or clothe her. The old nurse, when no one was by, would sometimes give her a dish of scraps from the kitchen, or a torn petticoat from the rag-bag, while the other servants of the palace would drive her from the house with blows and mocking words, calling her 'Tattercoats' and pointing at her bare feet and shoulders till she ran away crying, to hide among the bushes.

And so she grew up, with little to eat or wear, spending her days in the fields and lanes, with only the goose-herd for a companion, who would play to her so merrily on his little pipe when she was hungry, or cold, or tired, that she forgot all her troubles and fell to dancing with his flock of noisy geese for partners.

One day, people told each other that the King was travelling through the land, and in the town nearby was to give a great ball, to all the lords and ladies of the country, where the Prince, his only son, was to choose a wife.

One of the royal invitations was brought to the palace by the sea, and the servants carried it up to the old lord who still sat by his window, wrapped in his long white hair and weeping into the little river that was fed by his tears. But when he heard the King's command, he dried his eyes and bade them bring shears to cut him loose, for his hair had bound him a fast prisoner and he could not move. He then sent for rich clothes and jewels, and he ordered them to saddle the white horse with gold and silk, so that he might ride to meet the King.

Meanwhile, Tattercoats had heard of the great doings in the town, and she sat by the kitchen door weeping because she could not go to see them. When the old nurse heard her crying she went to the Lord of the Palace and begged him to take his granddaughter with him to the King's ball.

But he only frowned and told her to be silent, while the servants laughed and said, 'Tattercoats is happy in her rags, playing with the goose-herd, let her be – it is all she is fit for.'

For a second, and then a third time, the old nurse begged him to let the girl go with him, but she was answered with black looks and fierce words, till she was driven from the room by the jeering servants, with blows and mocking words.

Weeping over her ill-success, the old nurse went to look for Tattercoats, but the girl had been turned from the door by the cook, and had run away to tell her friend the goose-herd of how unhappy she was because she could not go to the King's ball.

But once the goose-herd had listened to her story, he bade her cheer up and proposed that they should go together to the town to see the King, and all the fine things; and when she looked sorrowfully down at her rags and bare feet, he played a note or two upon his pipe, so gay and merry, that she forgot all about her tears and her troubles, and before she well knew, the herdboy had taken her by the hand, and she, and he, and the geese before them, were dancing down the road towards the town.

Before they had gone very far, a handsome young man, splendidly dressed, rode up and stopped to ask the way to the castle where the King was staying; and when he found that they too were going thither, he got off his horse and walked beside them along the road.

The herdboy pulled out his pipe and played a low sweet tune, and the stranger looked again and again at Tattercoats' lovely face till he fell deeply in love with her, and begged her to marry him.

But she only laughed, and shook her golden head.

'You would be finely put to shame if you had a goose-girl for your wife!' said she. 'Go and ask one of the great ladies you will see tonight at the King's ball, and do not flout poor Tattercoats.'

But the more she refused him the sweeter the pipe played, and the deeper the young man fell in love, till at last he begged her, as a proof of his sincerity, to come that night at twelve, just as she was in her torn petticoat and bare feet, to the King's ball with the herdboy and his geese; he would dance with her before the King and the lords and ladies, and present her to them all as his dear and honoured bride.

So when night came, and the hall in the castle was full of light and music, and the lords and ladies were dancing before the King, just as the clock struck twelve, Tattercoats and the herdboy, followed by his flock of noisy geese, entered at the great doors and walked straight up the ballroom, while on either side the ladies whispered, the lords laughed, and the King seated at the far end stared in amazement.

But as they came in front of the throne, Tattercoats' lover rose from beside the King and came to meet her. Taking her by the hand, he kissed her thrice before them all and turned to the King.

'Father!' he said, for it was the Prince himself, 'I have made my choice, and here is my bride, the loveliest girl in all the land, and the sweetest as well!'

Before he had finished speaking, the herdboy put his pipe to his lips and played a few low notes that sounded like a bird singing far off in the woods. As he played, Tattercoats' rags were changed to shining robes sewn with glittering jewels, a golden crown lay upon her golden hair, and the flock of geese behind her became a crowd of dainty pages, bearing her long train.

As the King rose to greet her as his daughter, the trumpets sounded loudly in honour of the new princess, and the people outside in the street said to each other, 'Ah! Now the Prince has chosen for his wife the loveliest girl in all the land!'

But the goose-herd was never to be seen again, and no one knew what became of him; the old lord went home once more to his palace by the sea, for he could not stay at Court when he had sworn never to look on his granddaughter's face.

And so there he still sits by his window, if you could only see him, as you someday may, weeping more bitterly than ever as he looks out over the sea.

According to the printed notes of Joseph Jacobs, the tale was collected by Marie Balfour from 'a little girl named Sally Brown, when she lived in the Cars [*sic*] in Lincolnshire. Sally had got it from her mother, who worked for Mrs Balfour.'

I carried out a search of the family history records for Redbourne and found that there was a Sarah Allina Brown (Sally being the abbreviation of her name) living in the village at the time that Marie Balfour was living there. Her mother was a house servant and her father a farm servant. Sally was at the local school at the same time as Agnes Bratten, who I believe to be the teller of 'The Dead Moon' and 'Sam'l's Ghost' (part of 'Fred the Fool').

One of the key characters in the tale is a goose-herd. It is noticeable that geese were kept in vast quantities in the fens of Lincolnshire. They were bred not just for the flesh, which would feed many, but also for the feathers which were used for pillows and quill pens. The job of the goose-herd was to drive the whole flock from their habitations to water twice a day and return them safely. The goose-herd (or Gozzard, as he was often known in Lincolnshire) was often regarded as the lowest of the low amongst the 'herders', and as a consequence the term would also be used for a fool or an idiot.

8

LINCOLNSHIRE RIDDLES

Riddles are considered to be one of the oldest and most culturally widespread of folklore genres. They have also played an important part in popular stories since the earliest times, and are found in some of the stories within this book. Mabel Peacock collected a number of riddles from around the county. Here are a few of them:

Round the house,
And round the house,
And in at parlour window.
What's that?

Answer: Sunshine.

Creeps through the hedge and steals the corn,
Little cow with leather horns –
What is it?

Answer: A hare.

Under water, over water,
And never touches water –
What's that?

Answer: A lass going over a bridge with
a pail of water on her head.

I heard a great rumble,
As I was going over the Humber,
Three pots a boiling,
And no fire under –
What's that?

Answer: Water under the boat.

When I was going through a field of wheat,
I picked up something that's good to eat;
It wasn't fish, flesh, bird, nor bone,
I kept it till it ran alone.
What was it?

Answer: An egg.

As I went through our garden gap,
I met my Uncle Ned,
With pins and needles upon his back,
And he kept on jogging ahead –
What was he?

Answer: A pricky-orchin (hedgehog).

Round the house,
And round the house,
And leaves a white glove in the window.
What is it?

Answer: Snow.

Round the house,
And round the house,
And leaves a black glove in the window.
What is it?

Answer: Rain.

As black as ink, and isn't ink;
As white as milk, and isn't milk;
As soft as silk, and isn't silk;
And hops about like a filly foal –
What's this?

Answer: A magpie.

Mother, father, sister, brother,
All running after one another,
And can't catch one another.
What are they?

Answer: Mill sails.

Thirty white horses upon a red hill,
Now they go, now they go, now they stand still.
What are they?

Answer: Teeth.

Round the house,
And round the house,
And in the cupboard?
What is it?

Answer: A mouse.

A riddle, a riddle, as I suppose,
Fifty eyes and never a nose.
What am I?

Answer: A sieve.

It is in the oyster, but not in the shell;
It is in the clapper, but not in the bell;
It is in the church, but not in the steeple;
It is in the parson, but not in the people;
It is in the rock, but not in the stone;

It is in the marrow, but not in the bone;
It is in the bolster, but not in the bed;
It is not in the living, nor yet in the dead.
What is it?

Answer: The letter R.

SELECT
GLOSSARY OF
LINCOLNSHIRE WORDS

This glossary has been compiled to aid the understanding of the Lincolnshire dialect wincluded within some of the tales in this book. It is, therefore, limited in its content. For a comprehensive glossary of Lincolnshire words the best books to consult are Peacock (1889), Elder (1997) and Sims-Kimbrey (1996). For the few Yorkshire words found in the county, the online resource by Morris (1892) is useful.

Agur – ague (marsh fever, a form of malaria)

Arsy-varsy – topsy-turvy, head over heels, wrong end first

Bairns – young children

Boggart/boggard – Lincolnshire term for a hobgoblin or something of an unearthly nature. Ghost or apparition in Yorkshire

Bogles/boggles – general term in Lincolnshire for a ghost or apparition, or for a wetlands goblin

Born fool – unwise person

Brat – child

By and by – after a time, shortly

Chunter – to mutter

Dant – damn

Doorsill – threshold

Dyke – ditch or drain

Fairy ring – a circle in grass believed to be made by fairies dancing

Flit/flitted – move from one place to another

Fo'ak/folk – family

Girn – is a term used in Lincolnshire and Yorkshire for grinning

Gob/gob-hole – a term used for mouth

Hark – listen

Hout/hoot – 'nonsense 'surely not

Kirkgarth – churchyard

Lawks/laws – explanation of surprise

Martlemas/Martinmas – 23rd November

Mools – Yorkshire term used to mean moulds, earth, soil

Naw – no

Nobbut/nobut – nothing but, only

Nowt – nothing

Pyewipe – lapwing

Ramper – the high road, main road or highway

Ramper/ramp – to rush about violently, though in the case of these stories it seems to refer to being lively.

'Rampin' could be derived from the word 'rampant' as in heraldry, which can mean exuberant

Singing iron – firing or burning iron: an instrument with which horses are branded

Snag – a piece of wood projecting from the root of a tree or post that has been broken off

Stot – stumble

Tiddy – small

Todlowries – hobgoblins

Tussocks – tuft or bunch of coarse grass

Watter – water

Will-o'-the-Wykes/Will-o'-the-Wisp – *ignis fatuus*, the self-igniting marsh gas found in wetlands that appears as small flickering flames on the surface of the water. These flames were also known as jack o' lanterns

Yaller – yellow

Yule – was used to refer to Christmas in North Lincolnshire

BIBLIOGRAPHY

BOOKS AND ARTICLES

Addy, Sidney, *Household Tales and Traditional Remains* (London, David Nutt, 1895)

Balfour, Marie Clothilde, *Fall of the Sparrow* (London, Methuen & Co., 1897)

_____, 'Legends of the Carrs', *Folklore*, Vol. 2, No. 2 (June 1891) Vol. 2, No. 3 (Sept. 1891) No. 4 (Dec. 1891)

Briggs, Katharine, *A Dictionary of British Folk Legends in the English Language: Part A, Folk Narratives* (London, Routledge & K. Paul, 1969)

_____ *The Fairies in Tradition and Literature* (London, Routledge & K. Paul, 1967)

Briggs, Katharine & Ruth Tongue, *Folktales of England* (London, Routledge & Kegan Paul, 1965)

Clare, John, *The Rural Muse* (London, Whittaker & Co., 1835)

Ekirch, A. Roger, *At Days Close: A History of Nighttime* (London, Weidenfield & Nicholson, 2005)

Elder, Eileen (Ed.), *The Peacock Lincolnshire Word Books 1884–1920* (Scunthorpe Museum Society, 1997)

Forbes, Cora B., *Elizabeth's Charm String* (Boston, Little, Brown & Co., 1903)

Gee, Herbert, *Folk Tales of Yorkshire* (London, Thomas Nelson & Sons Ltd, 1953)

Gomme, A.B., *The Traditional Games of England Scotland & Ireland*, vol. 2 (London, David Nutt & Co., 1884)

Goodwin, Charles W. (Ed.), *Felix – Life of St Guthlac* (London, J.R. Smith, 1848)

Gutch, Edith & Mabel Peacock, *Examples of Printed Folk-Lore Concerning Lincolnshire, County Folk-Lore Vol. 5* (London, David Nutt, 1908)

Halliwell-Phillipps, James, *Popular Rhymes and Nursery Tales* (London, John Russell Smith, 1849)

Heywood, Simon, *The New Storytelling: A History of the Storytelling Movement in England and Wales* (Devon, Daylight Press for the Society for Storytelling, 1999)

Horn, D., 'Tiddy Mun's Curse and the Ecological Consequences of Land Reclamation', *Folklore*, vol. 98 (1987)

Hutton, Ronald, *The Rise and Fall of Merry England: The Ritual Year 1400–1700* (Oxford, Oxford University Press, 1994)

Jackson, Charles (Ed.), *The Diary of Abraham de la Pryme – The Yorkshire Antiquary* (Durham, Andrews & Co., 1870)

Jackson, Charles, 'The Stovin Manuscript', *The Yorkshire Archaeological Journal*, vol. 7 (London, Elliot Stock, 1882)

Jacobs, Joseph, *More English Fairy Tales* (London, David Nutt, 1894)

Kent, Edward George, *Lindum Lays and Legends* (London, Simpkin, Marshall & Co., 1861)

Kitchen, Fred, *Brother to the Ox – the Autobiography of a Farm Labourer* (London, J.M. Dent, 1940)

Lang, Andrew (Ed.), 'English and Scotch Fairy Tales', *Longman's Magazine*, vol. 15 (March 1890) and *Folklore*, vol. 1 (September 1890)

Marlowe, Christopher, *Legends of the Fenland People* (London, Cecil Palmer, 1926)

McNeaney, Sean, 'The Wild Man of Stainfield', *Lincolnshire Life* (February 2005)

Nichols, Beverley, *A Book of Old Ballads* (London, Hutchinson & Co., 1934)

Pacey, Robert (Ed.), *The Diary of Ethel Rudkin*, vol. I (Privately circulated publication, 2002)

Page, William (Ed.), 'Houses of Benedictine Monks: The Abbey of Crowland', *A History of the County of Lincoln*, vol. 2 (1906)

Peacock, Mabel, *Taales fra Linkisheere* (London, G. Jackson & Son, 1889)

_____, *Tales and Rhymes in Lindsey Folk-Speech* (London, G. Jackson & Son, 1886)

_____, 'The Folklore of Lincolnshire', *Folklore*, vol. 12, no. 2 (June, 1901)

_____, 'Notes on Professor J. Rhys's Manx Folk-Lore and Superstitions' in *Folklore* vol. 2, no. 4 (December 1891)

_____, 'Notes on the Lay of Havelok' reproduced in *Lincolnshire Life*, vol. 5, no. 5 (November/December, 1965)

Pearson, Ken, 'Yellowbelly Folklore', *Lincolnshire Life* (December 1998)

Philip, Neil, *Victorian Village Life* (Spring Hill, Albion Press, 1993)

Rawnsley, William, *Highways and Byways in Lincolnshire* (London, Macmillan & Co., 1914)

Robinson, David, *Book of Louth* (Buckingham, Barracuda Books, 1979)

Rudkin, Ethel, *Lincolnshire Folklore* (Gainsborough, Beltons, 1936)

———, 'Lincolnshire Folklore, Belief and Practice', *Folklore*, vol. 44, no. 2 (June 1933)

———, 'Lincolnshire Folklore, Witches and Devils', *Folklore*, vol. 45, no. 3 (September 1934)

Sternberg, Thomas, *The Dialect and Folk-Lore of Northamptonshire* (London, John Russell Smith, 1851)

Sutton, M., *A Lincolnshire Calendar* (Lincoln, Paul Watkins, 1997)

Thomas, Keith, *Religion and the Decline of Magic* (London, Penguin, 1991)

Tongue, Ruth, *Forgotten Folkores of the English Counties* (London: Routledge & K. Paul. 1970)

Walter, James, 'The Legend of Byard's Leap', *Bygone Lincolnshire* (Hull, A. Brown & Sons, 1891)

Waters, Richard, *The Lost Treasure of King John* (Grantham, Barny Books, 2003)

Westwood, J. and J. Simpson, *The Lore of the Land: A Guide to England's Legends* (London, Penguin Books, 2005)

Wynne, Meg, *Lincolnshire Folklore: Ghosts and Legends Galore!* (Louth, Allinson & Wilcox, 1976)

MAGAZINES AND NEWSPAPERS

Lincolnshire Echo
Northampton Mercury
The Gentleman's Magazine
The Lincolnshire Magazine
The Newcastle Courant

ABOUT
THE AUTHOR

Maureen James is an historian, writer, storyteller and teacher. She gained a passion for history as a result of reading a historical novel in 1985, and has since devoted much of her time to researching and spreading this passion by whatever means possible. Her education has since included undergraduate studies at Cambridge University, a Master's Degree at the University of London, and has recently been awarded the title of Doctor of Philosophy for her research into the 'Legends of the Carrs', which included work on the folklore, folk tales and storytellers of Lincolnshire. The spread of her love of the past has included museum education, living history presentations, talks, lectures and writing. She is also a regular contributor to *Smallholder Magazine* on the subject of history, folklore and folk customs. Maureen has, however, found that the most effective way to share her passion for things historical has been through the medium of the spoken voice, particularly telling historical stories that are evocative of mood, place and time. She often wears historical costume, and has told her stories, which are particularly from the Lincolnshire and Cambridge Fens, though her repertoire now includes many other British stories, at diverse venues including medieval manor houses, iron-age forts, castles and abbeys and even in a barn standing beside a lively Exmoor pony. More recently she has regularly been seen dressed as a Victorian folklorist spreading her knowledge of the subject at summer events, including the Heckington Show. For further information see her website, www.tellinghistory.com.

If you enjoyed this book, you may also be interested in …

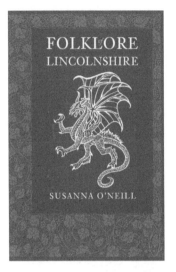

Folklore of Lincolnshire

SUSANNA O'NEILL

The county of Lincolnshire is a beautiful mixture of low-lying marshy fen land, modest hills and the steep valleys of the rolling Wolds; it is also home to a wealth of folklore, legend and intrigue. With one of the most interesting dialects in the country, this vast region is also rich in superstitions, songs and traditional games. A study of the daily life, lore and customs of Lincolnshire are here interspersed with stories of monstrous black hounds, dragon lairs, witches, Tiddy Mun, mischievous imps and tales of the people known as the Yellowbellies.

978 0 7524 5964 6

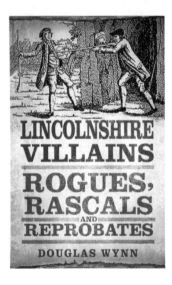

Lincolnshire Villains: Rogues, Rascals and Reprobates

DOUGLAS WYNN

In the past, the east shore of Lincolnshire's long coastline was well adapted for smuggling and the rural quality of the county aided the transport and hiding of contraband goods. In addition to the pirates, coastal criminals and countryside rogues, there was also murder and mayhem aplenty in such cities as Lincoln, Grimsby, Boston and Stamford. Moreover, being near to the north/south routes from London meant that Lincolnshire was a haven for highwaymen and footpads – even the infamous Dick Turpin had a connection to Lincolnshire.

978 0 7524 6611 8

Visit our website and discover thousands of other History Press books.

www.thehistorypress.co.uk